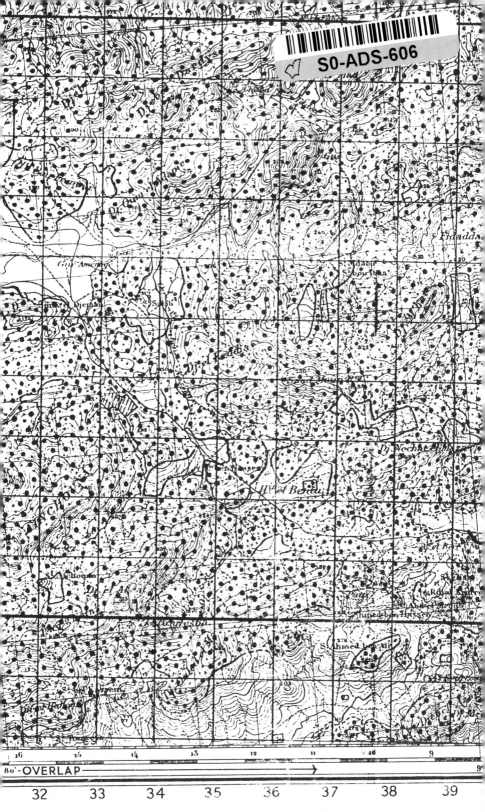

SEDJENANE: THE PAY-OFF BATTLE

for Carlo D'Este
with much appreciation
for your help + encouragement.
"Red" Phillips
9-22-93

SEDJENANE

The Pay-Off Battle

-》》-》》-》》《《-《《-《《-

Leading to the Capture of Bizerte, Tunisia, by the 9th U.S. Infantry Division, May 9, 1943

Henry Gerard Phillips

Preface by
General William C. Westmoreland

IN MEMORIUM

This book is dedicated to Sergeant William L. Nelson,
H Company, 60th Infantry, who was posthumously awarded the

MEDAL OF HONOR

CITATION: *For conspicuous gallantry and intrepidity at risk of life,
above and beyond the call of duty in action involving actual conflict at
Djebel Dardys, Northwest of Sedjenane, Tunisia. On the morning of 24
April, 1943, Sergeant Nelson led his section of heavy mortars to a forward position where he placed his guns and men. Under intense enemy
artillery, mortar and small arms fire, he advanced alone to a chosen
observation position from which he directed the laying of a concentrated
mortar barrage which successfully halted an initial enemy counterattack. Although mortally wounded in the accomplishment of his mission, and with his duty clearly completed, Sergeant Nelson crawled to a
still more advanced observation point and continued to direct the fire of
his section. Dying of hand grenade wounds and only fifty yards from the
enemy, Sergeant Nelson encouraged his section to continue their fire and
by so doing they took a heavy toll of enemy lives. The skill which Sergeant Nelson displayed in this engagement, his courage, and self-
sacrificing devotion to duty and heroism resulting in the loss of his life,
was a priceless inspiration to our Armed Forces and were in keeping
with the highest traditions of the Army of the United States.*

Contents

List of Illustrations

Preface

I put down Lieutenant Colonel Phillips' earlier book, *El Guettar: Crucible of Leadership,* with disappointment that he had not extended the story of the 9th Infantry Division in Africa to show how quickly it absorbed the lessons of that battle and carried on to victory in Northern Tunisia. He has done it now with *Sedjenane: the Pay-off Battle* and it is a fascinating analysis of maneuver's advantages over the deceptively simple direct approach to a military objective.

More than a review of different tactics, however, Phillips has carefully studied the leadership style of one of World War II's most successful corps commanders whose attributes to this point have been largely neglected by biographers. Manton S. Eddy was an unusually gifted tactician and a consummate combat leader. Most of this he learned as we progressed through Africa and Europe. He was resilient and never made the same error twice.

As an artillery battalion commander in the 9th and later artillery executive officer, I was witness to General Eddy's manner of getting the most from his people. He was a great believer in giving responsibility with a loose rein. He was the epitome of patience when he believed an honest effort had been made. The result of this was the generation of great loyalty, devotion and perseverence among his subordinates.

"Red" Phillips' two books make a package that should be on every professional soldier's bookshelf.

William C. Westmoreland

Charleston, South Carolina.

Introduction

El Guettar: Crucible of Leadership concluded with the 9th Infantry Division laying sprawled near exhaustion across Hill 369, its objective. A faint trace of dust hanging in the air to the northeast was all that remained of the enemy. It was a conceded victory not to be compared with the bell-ringer that would come just a month later. "Why did you stop there," a great many asked. "Why didn't you continue to show how we learned something from that awful experience?"

That was the inspiration for this sequel. Perhaps another, subconscious reason for my stopping earlier was that, having been wounded and evacuated at El Guettar, I was not around for the campaign's glorious conclusion. Egotistically, I did not understand then that oral history is mostly the work of its contributors, not the editor. By the time *El Guettar* was finished, I knew who really wrote the book.

Those owed my special gratitude are identified in these pages with their contributions. Beyond this, I acknowledge a further debt to the following who were good enough to review chapter drafts and make valued comments and suggestions: Col. (Ret.) Arden C. Brill, Col. (Ret.) Robert B. Cobb, Col. (Ret.) Herbert E. Clark, Col. (Ret.) George I. Connolly, Col. (Ret.) Jack A. Dunlap. Col. (Ret.) Alex T. Forrest, Brig. Gen. (Ret.) Frank L. Gunn, Col. (Ret.) Donald L. Harrison, Lt. Col. (Ret.) William H. Horan, Col. (Ret.) Ray Inzer, Col. (Ret.) Richard F. Kent, Col. (Ret.) H. W. Lange, Brig. Gen. (Ret.) Lewis E. Maness, Lt. Col. (Ret.) John W. Miller, Col. (Ret.) Duncan W. Murphy, Col. (Ret.) H. Price Tucker, Col. (Ret.) Dean T. Vanderhoef, Lt. Col. (Ret.) Bert C. Waller and Col. (Ret.) John J. Wessmiller and Gen. (Ret.) William C. Westmoreland.

Also, I thank Robert H. Pettee and Herbert U. Stern for their translations, Mrs. Imogene Stroh Stumpf for access to her father's papers and Maj. Gens. (Ret.) Michael B. Kauffman and Robert J. Hennen, as well as the able military historian Carlo W. D'Este for their generous endorsements of the final product.

Finally, there are those whose contributions to this book are remarkable because they were not there with us and so had nothing personal to gain by helping to improve the record. I refer here to my wife Lee, the editor's editor; to my mentor, the admirable historian Martin Blumenson; to Dr. Ernst Breitenberger and our friends in Germany, and the historian James Lucas in England, who helped with marvelous insight to find veterans of our battle from the other side.

"Red" Phillips

Lake Wildwood, California

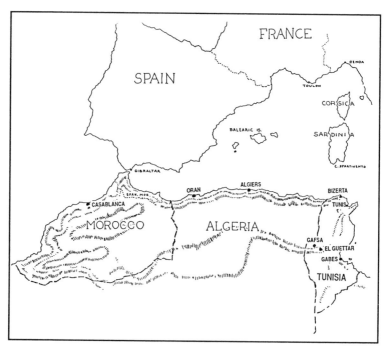

Map 1. General map of region.

A NEW MISSION

The big man with twin silver stars on each shoulder descended from his command car and squinted down the road to the east where, in brilliant sunshine, units of Randle's 47th were forming their convoy. It was still a worry whether the Luftwaffe would pick up the midday movement and come to strafe and bomb El Guettar's survivors. Maybe his men would get a break this time. The German pilots had taken a whipping toward the end of the battle just finished. As if responding to provide reassurance, a pair of American P-39s broke over the northern mountains and began to patrol the valley. The general smiled.

Major General Manton S. Eddy's 9th Infantry Division was going right back into it. Even before their committment to the Battle of El Guettar they had received orders to join the British First Army in northern Tunisia for its scheduled attack on Bizerte and Tunis. General Patton, urged on by his deputy (soon to be his successor) Omar Bradley, protested dismemberment of II U.S. Corps and Eisenhower ruled that the Americans would all fight together in the north under an American commander (to be Bradley when Patton returned to Algeria to continue planning the Sicilian invasion.) The entire American force, then, would have to cross behind the XIX French Corps and First British Army and reestablish itself along the Mediterranean shore. Shortly after noon on April 8th the 47th Infantry Regiment became the first element of what would evolve as a major logistic reorganization and strategic movement.

Major General Manton S. Eddy,
Commanding General, 9th Infantry Division.
(Army Signal Corps photo.)

A jeep detached itself from the huge dust cloud rising from the 47th's assembly area and headed west along the macadam road toward the high point where the general was watching. It was Randle, the 47th's commander and one of the stars of the battle just finished. Eddy knew Randle had made some mistakes but these were more than balanced by his results. The colonel was cool under pressure and brave under fire. His men trusted him and willingly stuck out their necks when they thought it was what he wanted. It did not get much better than that.

The general had a great affinity for this subordinate who at 48 was three years his junior. They had been infantry company commanders in France at the same time and both had been wounded in action. Later, they were outsiders in the peacetime Regular Army whose officer corps was made up mostly of West Point graduates. While the other two regimental commanders were not West Point graduates either, they were not in the same ballpark as Randle in appearance, manner or leadership ability. Eddy would soon lose the 47th's C.O.(commanding officer), even if the enemy up north did not get him first. The general had recommended that Randle be promoted and when that worked its way back to the War Department, there would be orders transferring him out of the 9th to one of the new divisions forming back in the States. But there would be time to tell him about that later. This roadside was not the place.

The two officers exchanged salutes and small talk about the planes overhead. Then the general focused the conversation on the Division's new mission.

Eddy already had the recommendations of his assistant division commander who had been on the ground up north talking to the British they would relieve and to the operations people of the British First Army. Don Stroh was pushing for a holding attack by one of the 9th's three regiments against the main German defenses on two hills west of the village of Jefna, then using the division's other two regiments to flank those positions to the north. The hill positions blocked the principal and most direct approach to Bizerte.

Stroh reported how the British had previously attacked Green and Bald Hills, as they had named them, directly without success. The Germans had well-prepared positions and plenty of firepower. Another head-on attack of these hills would be a re-run of what the 9th had just been through at El Guettar, slowly grinding away against determined defenders possessing adequate means and superior observation.

'We gotta hold 'em by the nose with one regiment and kick 'em in the tail with the others,' Stroh suggested with a grin at this

-3-

reminder of General Patton. 'One of our envelopments should be shallow and add to the threat of Jefna.' he explained, 'The other would go in further north and strike deeper, cutting the Germans' means of supporting the Jefna defenses.'

'What about the Kraut's reserves?' Eddy asked.

Stroh replied that the Germans were going to be stretched thin when the entire Allied force struck together across their front:

'The British will kick off a day ahead of us and the enemy won't have anything left with which to counterattack. With our attachments we'll have them outnumbered four-and-a-half to one and our advantage in guns is even greater,' Stroh asserted. 'We'll smother them.'

Eddy worried that his assistant might be underestimating the enemy. Attacking or defending, the Germans almost always held back a reserve, and they could be depended upon to counterattack. Committing everything at the outset cut across the grain of everything the general had been taught in the Army's service schools, or that he had taught others. "Two up and one back" was a tactical axiom, but sometimes exceptions were acceptable and this could be such. It all depended upon that holding attack. At first it had to look like the main effort. After that it had to be serious enough to keep the German commander plagued by the "what ifs."

In its sector the 9th would oppose two mixed-bag regiments of the German Division von Manteuffel which, with attachments, had a strength of about 5,000 organized into nine battalion-size combat units. One fifth of these men were Italians. Totaling 22,500 men with attachments, Eddy was sure that his unit could smother the enemy unless they brought in something else. The remainder of the Manteuffel Division was facing adjacent British units to the south and the General was confident that they would do their best to keep the Germans busy. Eddy's intelligence experience, however, warned him that his G2 should give special attention to what was going on south of the Division's boundary as well as behind the lines as the battle unfolded.

British intelligence passed to the 9th was detailed and thorough. Most of the enemy's frontline units and artillery positions were plotted and defined. The man for whom the opposing division was named (itself an indication that it might lack conventional support elements), Generalmajor Hasso E. von Manteuffel was a veteran of fighting in Poland, France and Russia.[1] While the 9th had the edge in manpower and supporting weapons, Eddy realized that he was up against a foe who knew the battlefield intimately and who was capable of taking full advantage of any of the attacker's mistakes. Division Manteuffel was battle-tested. It played a major part in the German offensive in north-ern Tunisia from February 26th to March 15th, which drove back the British 46th Infantry Division and the French Corps Franc d'Afrique from the positons they now held to the town of Djebel Abiod, about 15 miles west of Sedjenane. Then the Allies pushed the Germans back to their original strongholds around Jefna. Some of the German's losses had been replaced. Now they were digging and waiting.

Ordinarily a commander faced with Eddy's tactical dilemma might economize and use his weakest element to conduct a feint or holding attack. In this instance, however, with so much depending upon the success of his ploy, it only seemed reasonable for the division commander to use his strongest and most dependable regiment, the 47th Infantry, at this critical point.

Eddy summarized his thinking and passed on his conclusions to Randle:

> *'It's not going to be easy,' he cautioned. 'You're going to have to patrol vigorously around the clock. Your company command-ers must be inspired to act independently. They'll have to grab prisoners for interrogation so that we know what's going on over on the far side.'*

Randle assured his commander that the 47th had been the right choice to make the holding attack. Since by this time the first ele-ments of his convoy were moving onto the highway, the Colonel excused himself to check their timing and appearance.

Eddy continued to muse over the tactical proposal for the Divi-sion's opening the way to Bizerte. A two-pronged envelopment plus the absence of a reserve made it a risky venture. Patton would go for it in a minute, but how would Bradley view the departure from "two up and one back?" It was hard to guess. The two men were barely acquainted. Bradley had no World War I combat experience and, while Eddy and he had been at Fort Benning, Georgia at the same time, their assignments at The Infantry School had not overlapped. Bradley had no part of the African landings either. It was never easy breaking in a new boss but more so when you couldn't quite get a handle on the man.

Eddy returned to the more immediate problem. Which envelop-ment was the more critical and who should make it: Colonel J. Trimble Brown with his 39th Infantry or Colonel Frederic J. de Rohan with the 60th?

For the first time the 60th Infantry would be fighting as a part of the 9th under Eddy's command. On the other hand, the 39th's com-mander had become well-known to the General in the short time that

Generalmajor Hasso E. von Manteuffel,
Commanding General, Manteuffel Division.
(From the collection of Don E. Burkel.)

regiment had been back as part of his command. At El Guettar, Brown had been extremely argumentative about Eddy's piecemeal employment of his battalions and even abusive to his commander about the ill-fated Oake's mission. Eddy was determined there would be no more of that. Brown had been warned; the next time would be the last.[2]

Frederic J. de Rohan, on the other hand, was relatively unknown. While there had been rumors that the 60th's landing operation at Port Lyautey had been mismanaged, nothing official had come down. Even if true, the problem may not have been de Rohan's fault. Assault landings on hostile shores were fraught with unexpected calamities due to the services' inexperience with working together, as well as surprises about the enemy and his arena. In the final analysis, the 60th had prevailed at Port Lyautey.

Then, while the 9th Division was attacking at El Guettar, its 60th Infantry was attached to the 1st Armored Division attacking at Maknassy, 50 miles away. As the number of the Regiment's casualties showed, the fighting there had been tough too. 1st Armored's staff had no serious complaints about its attached "straight-leg" infantry but Patton had fired its commander before Eddy had had a chance to talk to him about de Rohan's performance.

For these reasons then, and assuming Stroh's scheme would be approved by higher headquarters, Eddy opted to use the 39th nearer home on the shorter rein. While the 60th's wide-flanking maneuver would be trickier, it would be less critical to accomplishing the Division's mission. If the 60th failed, the 9th might still succeed through actions of its other regiments. If the 60th were successful it might pay off spectacularly, but it would be icing on the cake.

The big man cracked his fist into the palm of his other hand. He turned and jumped in back of the command car. "Let's go home," he ordered. The General was ready to present his concept of the forthcoming operation to the staff and get them working out the details.

Notes

1. After von Manteuffel was evacuated as sick at the close of the Tunisian campaign, he rose to great heights in the Wehrmacht and was one of the architects of the Ardennes offensive.

2. Having landed near Algiers on November 8th the 39th's commander at the time was promoted and reassigned. Brown, the regi-

ment's executive officer, was given command and promoted. After the landing, the 39th was split up guarding lines of communication to Tunisia and parts were mauled in Rommel's February offensive. The regiment did not reassemble and rejoin the 9th until the division's arrival in Tunisia early in March, 1943.

The Oakes mission was a vain hope involving the 2nd Bn., 39th Inf., which was meant to catch the enemy asleep early in the El Guettar battle. The maneuver failed and casualties were heavy, including capture of the battalion commander, Lt. Col. Walter M. Oakes.

MOVING NORTH

Today Bou Chebka is a minor customs post on the Algerian-Tunisian border, but in 1943 it was a hot corner, figuring importantly in the Battle of Kasserine Pass and thereafter as an assembly area for II Corps forces moving to the front. Facilities were maintained at Bou Chebka where soldiers could rest, clean up and resupply. The Tebessa area supply bases were handy. It became the funnel through which the 9th Infantry Division, followed by much of the remaining II Corps forces, would enter the routes chosen to cross the French and British lines of communication enroute to its new area of operations in Northern Tunisia.

In turn, the 47th, the 39th, 9th Division Artillery and division special troops pulled back to Bou Chebka from El Guettar, followed by the 60th Regimental Combat Team from Maknassy, all spreading out in the scrub of the plateau country and digging still another slit trench if none was available from previous tenants. Tents went up and rations from the big cans rather than the little ones were warmed. Delicious-tasting bread was issued. Letters from home were handed out, with embarassed silence when the mail clerk called the name of someone who would never get another wish for his continued well-being. Citations got written, broken or worn-out equipment replaced and, greatest of all Bou Chebka's blessings, companies headed for the showers where there was lots of hot water and soap, and, after that, clean uniforms.

Staff Sergeant Wilfred M. Thornton, M Company, 60th Infantry, remembers about Bou Chebka that the hot shower was only from a GI can rigged up in the back of a truck, but it was the first he had in 51 days and felt "like heaven." Thornton's uniform was past redemption and went on a bonfire after an on-the-spot issue of clean clothes.

Bou Chebka by night even offered entertainment. After so much time on the line, Special Services could actually come up with a movie which no one had seen before. Or, perhaps one of the combo units of the Division Band came by to play a few numbers. If they failed to show, volunteers were always ready to sing for their buddies. Leisure brought an upsurge of emotions usually surpressed in battle or ignored on the long slogging marches. Feelings ranged from relief and camaraderie, through satisfaction and confidence to, in some cases, deep despair. The chaplains had great runs from the grateful and also from those few who realized that more horror was to come and soon.

Pfc. Charles E. Hoffman, B Company, 15th Engineers, remembers an exception to the steady diet of canned food that came to the troops at Bou Chebka. Reportedly, General Patton, now in his final week as commander of II Corps, arranged an issue of beefsteak to the 9th Division in appreciation for its services at El Guettar and Maknassy.

Staff Sergeant Robert E. McCully, L Company, 47th Infantry, recalls Patton walking through the area past his puptent. "We did not know who he was until someone spotted those pearl handles on his pistols. We felt it was a compliment that he visited us."

A major task facing the 47th Infantry's commanding officer during its stay at Bou Chebka was reconstituting E Company which had been lost, almost totally, in the recent battle.

lst Lieutenant William B. Larson of the 47th remembers:

> *Shortly after the Battle of El Guettar ended I was told to report to Colonel Randle. He opened up telling me how there was nothing left of E Company except for a few cooks and the supply sergeant, and that it must be rebuilt immediately. NCOs (non-commissioned officers) from the 1st and 3rd Battalions were being transferred as a cadre. Additional replacements would begin arriving the next day. He said that I was appointed the commander and I could have my pick of one other lieutenant of the regiment to be second-in-command. The other officers would be selected from the replacements due the next day. Finally, he said I would have a minimum of two to three weeks in which to organize and train the new company for combat.*
>
> *The next few days were a nightmare--getting 133 new men organized and equipped, instilling discipline, testing non-coms. We started each day with an Officer's Call to answer questions about the schedule. Every afternoon I would meet with the NCOs to do the same. These meetings were brief but gave all of us a chance to know one another and to pass on background and experience whether it be from training or the battlefield.*
>
> *Inside the deadline I could tell that with our combination of experienced and 'green' NCOs and officers, together with high-spirited troops, we were making progress. I could only hope that the next fight would show we made the right choices. There was no doubt that my selection of Jim Leopold as executive officer had been right. He was my mainstay.*

Control of the movement of II US Corps across the rear of the Allies was a finely-tuned thing, a classic example for teaching at the war colleges of many nations. But the 9th Division was the pathfinder. Its staff worked with the British movement control specialists to bring north-bound convoys across the heavy front-headed supply traffic with few interruptions. Organization, timing and discipline were the keynotes. Convoy elements had to hit the start points as scheduled, maintain prescribed speed and distances between vehicles and follow prearranged procedures for clearing obstacles. The 9th's experience making the long march across Algeria from Morocco paid big dividends.

The 9th moved from Tebessa north to Souk Ahras and thence northeastward through Le Terf, Roum es Souk, Tabarka and Djebel Abiod. From Le Terf the way merged with one of the principal east-west supply routes, making coordination especially tricky. On April 12th the 47th Infantry moved through the night to relieve the 138th Brigade of the British 46th Infantry Division east of Sedjenane.

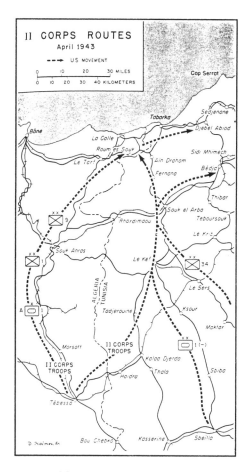

Map 2 Routes to the north.
(From Northwest Africa: Seizing the Initiative in the West.)

-11-

Depending upon weather conditions and the time of day that units moved, the 200-mile motor march was a pleasant outing or a time of some anxiety. Master Sergeant Fred A. Abben, the 47th's operations sergeant, wrote home about the people of the countryside walking along the sides of the road in their Sunday best:

> *It didn't seem like a war at all. They were friendly in their greetings and full of smiles. It was getting warm. Spring seemed to be in the air. At first the treeless slopes of the hills and valleys were covered with gay flowers, brilliant in their reds and yellows. Many were just tiny creations but they grew in such profusion that they formed almost continual carpets of color. Further north, heavy green underbrush bordered the road while on each side big eroded ridges extended upwards.*

2nd Lieutenant Jack A. Dunlap of B Company, 39th Infantry:

> *I joined the company as a replacement officer in the final days of the El Guettar fighting. I recall that clandestine movement to the Sedjenane valley, most of which was during darkness and across the British supply lines. The roads were narrow and treacherous and spanned steep escarpments and gorges.*

Private Warren E. Evans of A Company, 47th Infantry, recalls:

> *The Germans had blown up many of the bridges and at times we detoured through water and crawled up steep embankments. Sometimes the 6x6's leaned over so far we feared they might tip over and roll down the mountainside.*

lst Lieutenant Karl H. Ingebretsen, the 60th Infantry's transportation officer, recalls:

> *The night drives in the course of the move to Northern Tunisia were something to remember. It seems that the entire Tunisian campaign was taught to us at night. When we arrived up there some of the close-up supply points were weird. Besides our own men, food and ammo, we provided transport to the French and the Goums with their supplies of liquor and hay.*

Sergeant Gordon E. Herwig, A Company, 47th Infantry, recollects the following:

> *The convoy north was long and tiring for us dogface GIs. All we knew was that we were headed somewhere in a hurry. Speculation had it that we were going into a big show against Jerry. Luckily our trucks had canvas covers and we were protected against some of the dust. Latrine stops were few and far*

between for the military police riding shotgun were constantly pushing our convoy forward with cries to the drivers to 'close the gap!' There was constant conversation about our 'tonsils float-ing.' When the convoy stopped the men let fly over the tail gate. The platoon leader was furious and demanded more discipline.

We were on those trucks about 48 hours. I sat at the end of the bench by the tailgate. I learned to sleep with my rifle butt on the floor between my legs, barrel clasped in both hands at the knees and my chin resting on my forearms. Heavy jolts would partially wake me.

During the second day I noticed a change of scenery. Now the nearby hills were green and pleasant looking. Only once did we stop at a road crossing to let a Limey convoy pass to the east. We were on 'full speed ahead!'

Finally we unloaded and stretched out on our raincoats for a short snooze while the platoon leader and platoon sergeant reported for orders. When they returned we were given the big picture for our regiment and division. We were told that for the moment we were part of the British First Army but that, when we kicked off, the 9th would be part of an 'All American' offensive under II U.S. Corps.

Next came a run-through of what our outfit was to do. First we'd take over some British positions in the hills to the east. Then the 47th's 1st and 2nd Battalions would harass the large hill mass up ahead called Bald Hill while the 3rd Battalion flanked Green Hill to the northeast. These hills blocked the way to the town of Jefna further east along the road we'd come in on, and past that was the Division's objective, the city of Mateur.

Our immediate orders were to get ready to move in ten min-utes. Guides from the British outfit we were replacing had arrived to lead us up to their positions. It was a long walk and after a bit we could see Green and Bald Hills more clearly. There seemed to be a whole series of hills between us and them. We finally stopped on top of one and exchanged places with the Tommies. Everyone wished each other good luck. They advised us to stay out of the wadis and off the skyline as the Germans had these zeroed in with mortars and 88s. After El Guettar we expected this. One of the Limeys told our platoon sergeant that they had assaulted Bald Hill three times, each time withdrawing in a 'bloody mess.'

And from the notebook of lst Lieutenant Louis M. Prince, B Battery, 60th Field Artillery Battalion:

<u>Saturday, April 17th, 1943.</u> Here we are all ready to go into action again tonight. We moved up here yesterday and last night, near La Calle, Algeria, on the Mediterranean which is just as blue as in the technicolor movies. The water certainly felt good.

Tonight we move forward to the front lines where the whole 9th Division will relieve some English division which is holding the northernmost district near Bizerte. Bizerte and Tunis are the only parts the Germans have left, and they are said to be evacuating troops at the rate of 8,000 men a day, and the Royal Navy is supposed to be sinking most of them. But the German's Luftwaffe is still very active from Sicily and Sardinia as we noticed yesterday when we were attacked twice, and the town of Souk el Arba was bombed by 15 JU 87s just as we entered it. (No damage or casualties to us.)

Tonight we are in general support of the 47th and 39th Infantry as the 60th Infantry is in reserve. There will be lots of corps artillery like at Maknassy, the 17th and 36th plus the 84th, 34th and 26th of the 9th Division, so there will be plenty of noise as usual. Thank heavens the Germans don't use as much artillery as we do. It would be awful.

Thanks to the long advanced notice given the 9th's transfer to Northern Tunisia there had been much planning for turning over responsibility of the sector from the British 46th Infantry Division. The 9th's advance party had been on the ground with the British forward elements, the 138th Infantry and lst Parachute Brigades, since before the 9th's committment to the El Guettar offensive. Accordingly, all of the prior experience of the 46th with the terrain and the opposition, the German Division Manteuffel, had been made available to the Americans. They learned of the German positions and strengths, minefields and other obstacles and patrol patterns. Also important, there was time to know and assess a significant attachment to the 9th for the new offensive, the French Corps Franc d'Afrique.

France's colonial military establishment in North Africa was originally loyal in the extreme to Marshal Petain and his government in Vichy, France. Since they despised the British for their earlier attacks upon French naval units at Dakar and Oran, it was a delicate task for General Eisenhower to win over French support for the Allied undertaking in Northwest Africa. Those few French officers who had decided to cooperate with the Americans prior to the November 8th invasion were treated as traitors by most of their fellows. Only Eisenhower's direct intervention kept some from being shot. Gradually, the bulk of the French military was brought around to taking part in the campaign to rid their African territories of Axis forces. To do this they had to be rearmed and reequipped but, eventually, the French XIX Corps, including three infantry divisions and a tank battalion, took its place on the line in Tunisia. Quite apart from this metamorphosis was the creation and deployment of the Corps Franc d'Afrique (CFA). Led by some of those dissident officers who had been in contact with the Americans before the invasion, the CFA was made up of volunteers who, for various reasons, were in trouble with the authorities in Algiers, or who were disqualified from joining the regular forces because of race, citizenship or prison records. Its founders begged scraps of uniforms, arms and equipment and made their way to Tunisia where the British First Army allowed it an independent role and sector covering the Mediterranean shore. Here the CFA was able to tie down some weaker parts of the German Division Manteuffel.

By the time the 9th Infantry Division arrived in Northern Tunisia, it had been mutually agreed by all parties that the CFA would be under General Eddy's command. The pay-back for the 4,500-man CFA was that it would receive greater combat and logistic support than it had previously enjoyed. Captain Frank R. Veale, the 9th's Assistant G4, made arrangements with the British to barge supplies to the CFA down the coast from Bone, Algeria, to Cap Serrat. This saved traffic on the limited road from Sedjenane to Cap Serrat.

The CFA, then led by Colonel Pierre J. Magnan, was organized into four battalions of infantry and one of marines, but their most fascinating units were several tabours of Goumiers. Goumiers, or "Goums," as they were more broadly but incorrectly known, were Berber tribesmen who acted as scouts. Tough and fierce-looking, they were completely at ease in the wild, jungle-like environment of Northern Tunisia. These irregulars were allegedly paid according to the number of ears they collected from the German or Italian enemy. As an official procedure this has been denied by French authorities who acknowledge, however, that these mercenaries traditionally have been permitted to loot for their compensation. The official French line is that the Goumier's interest in ears only emerged from the American soldier's interest in them as souvenirs.

Tabours were loosely composed of 12 to 16 men led by a French NCO, frequently a Foreign Legionnaire. Goumiers were recruited from the hill tribes across French North Africa and often brought their families into the field with them. These natives were skilled huntsmen on any type of terrain. With primitive weapons they had learned the hard way how to close silently on their prey.

Goum irregular of Corps Franc d'Afrique.
(Army Signal Corps photograph.)

About the Goumiers, Sergeant Herbert U. Stern, an interrogator detailed to the 9th's G2 Section, recalls:

At one time I was temporarily assigned to a small Goum outfit headed by a French noncom. One day I watched an officer conduct weapons inspection. When he spotted something he didn't like he would pull his small stick from under his arm and beat the Berber warrior with it across the face, getting no reaction at all. Now I had heard rumors about the Goums infiltrating enemy positions and cutting off the ears of soldiers they found asleep and killed. The story was that they were paid based upon this proof of their prowess. I actually saw a couple of the men with what looked like ears tied to their ammunition belts.

Their eating habits were fascinating. They would kill a goat by cutting its throat. Then they'd hang it head up and one man would blow in air through a slit made in the neck while another peeled the skin off. Their favorite pieces were the heart and liver roasted on a stick over an open fire. How could anyone relish C-rations after that?

Pfc. Trevor Jones of the 9th Quartermaster Company remembers:

> *The Goums were crazy to get hold of a Thompson submachine gun since the old-time, long French jobs they had were cumbersome in thick cover. One day we hauled to a supply point where a gang of these Berber natives were distributing rations. I was carrying a Tommy gun and the top dog of this outfit made it clear that he wanted it. Nothing he offered interested me and I couldn't wait to get clear of there. I can still see that ugly fellow's pocked face with no teeth, stinking breath and a long, greasy pig-tail. He wore a torn, filthy robe and sandals made from old tires. There was no doubt in my mind that, if I didn't get out of there before dark, he was going to slit my throat just to get that weapon and its ammo.*

Sergeant Frank Brusic, D Company, 47th Infantry:

> *One day I climbed up ahead by myself and was observing our mortar fire when I felt a tap on my shoulder. A squad of Goums was there. They all had their strings of human ears hanging from their belts. It scared the hell out of me but I offered a smoke and that satisfied them.*

At least one Goumier had graduated from ear collecting. 1st Lieutenant Charles Scheffel. A Company, 39th Infantry, recalls:

> *While we were waiting to attack I came across one of the British officers left behind to show us the ropes. He had a Goum bodyguard with him all dressed in the native costume. In conversation the Brit asked if I had any gold teeth, but he stopped me when I started to show where I had a gold filling in my mouth. He told me never to smile too much in the presence of a Goum and then had his man show me a sack of gold chunks, presumably taken by 'field dentistry' from dead enemy.*

It was not only those in contact with the frontline Goumiers who remember them well, for example, Assistant G2 Dean T. Vanderhoef:

> *General Eddy seemed to think that my earlier two years studying French as a West Point cadet made me an accomplished linguist. For example, one day I was with the general and the Goum quartermaster on the matter of their rations--wine, live goats and cous cous. Communication was very poor but gradually improved as I scraped the moss off my French. Our leader was listening intently and heard the Goum say, 'Je demand. . .' at which time the general, tired of the whole thing, stated most*

firmly to me: 'You tell that character he is not about to demand anything!' It took a while to explain that the French verb 'demand' meant to request something.

The Goumiers and the rest of the CFA were a magnet for the war correspondents gathering to cover the next Allied offensive. While a tight security blanket had been thrown over the troops getting organized for this event, the CFA was not changing its location, strength or mission, so it was fair game. Among the correspondents assembled was a particularly gifted and evocative writer, A. J. Liebling, who wrote for *The New Yorker* magazine. Liebling described the CFA's sector and the only road that traversed it, a 20-mile long, one-lane, dirt track that connected the coast at Cap Serrat with the town of Sedjenane:[1]

> *... the country it runs through is covered with small hills and almost all the hills are covered with a ten-foot growth of tall bushes and short trees, so close together that once you leave the road you can't see fifty feet in front of you. From the top of any hill you can see the top of another hill, but, because of the growth, you can't tell whether there are men on it. This made the country hard to fight in. The hillsides that have no trees are bright with wildflowers in the spring.*

This dirt road was the main overland supply route of the CFA and later, when they became engaged, of the 9th's maneuvering elements and their supporting artillery. As this was building up, Liebling and his cohorts would follow along in the bumber-to-bumper, stop-and-go traffic and fill column after column with their observations and experiences.

One day Liebling came across 1st Lieutenant Carl Ruff of the 60th Infantry who was a liaison officer to the CFA. Ruff and a detail of 60th soldiers had just recovered the body of one of their men killed while doing some extracurricular fighting alongside the Goumiers. This was the astonishing Private Karl "Molotov" Warner whose combat derring-do extended back to the 60th's landing at Morocco.

Liebling was intrigued by what he learned of this colorful soldier whose body now lay at his feet and who had hailed from Liebling's home base. He later visited Warner's unit and learned more about him. Thus began his extensive investigation leading back to the streets of lower Manhattan and culminating with a poignant story that came out in *The New Yorker,* and later as the lead story of his collection, *Quest for Mollie and Other War Stories.*

Liebling took note of another American in CFA territory, Captain Alfred Yankauer, a combat surgeon of the 51st Medical Battalion, who had been assigned to help the French. What the doctor remembers of those days gives additional insight to the CFA's character:

> *I suppose I got this detail because I could speak a little French. I remember my first visit to their headquarters in the forest. The road was muddy and we got stuck. I was riding with a 60-year-old French nurse and when a group of fierce-looking men in bathrobes came out of the woods, Madame de Nobrega told me not to worry, they were French Berbers, 'Goumiers.' She spoke to them and they lifted the jeep, with all of us in it, out of the mud and onto firm ground.*
>
> *Madame de Nobrega was only one af many extraordinary people who made up the Corps Franc d'Afrique. She had served as a nurse during World War I and then married a Brazilian. She lived in his country and raised a family. When our war started she returned to France and volunteered her services. After the defeat in 1940 she managed to come to North Africa and was in jail for subversive activity when the Allies landed. Almost the entire Corps was made up of such oddballs. I recall a German communist and a Spanish priest, both of whom had fought Franco.*
>
> *Madame de Nobrega was the most interesting of them all. Everyone called her 'Grandmere' and indeed she was a grandmother. She had severe arthritis for which she took quantities of aspirin daily, but she was as active as a much younger woman and served quite close to the fighting. I'm sorry that I lost track of her after the war.*

American war correspondent Tom Henry reflected after the war that the attachment of the Goumiers to the 9th, with their tactics and ear-slicing reputation, "added immensely to the aura of mystery which enveloped the 9th as its regiments seemed to materialize out of darkness and vanish into darkness again."[2]

For nearly everyone in the 9th Division the change from southern to northern Tunisia was felt to be dramatic. It called for different ways of doing things. Add to this its being highlighted by the sudden change of command of II U.S. Corps.

2nd Lieutenant George I. Connolly, a forward observer of the 34th Field Artillery Battalion, recalls:

> *Valleys up north frequently had water in them and were covered thickly with a brush or cane which made a machete necessary to make cross country progress. We thought about what we*

had heard of the South Pacific area. One man in the lead of a column hacking away, the rest following single file and relieving the cutter periodically. The hills were as bad but up here there was some concealment under trees. The defenders still had the observation.

Perhaps the best comment about the differences of northern and southern Tunisia was made by Lieutenant Paul Lynch of the 39th. He noted that at El Guettar every doughboy was looking to swap his M1 for an '03 rifle for its advantage of range and accuracy. In the Sedjenane area he was doing everything he could to arm himself with a Tommy gun.

Everyone was very careful to proceed up or down ridgelines while staying off the skyline itself. I remember Frank Gunn repeating, 'Stay off that skyline or we'll all get killed.'

Just as the terrain was different, so was the climate. The humidity up north wore you out. When Omar Bradley took command of II Corps the first thing he did was to lift the requirement to wear neckties and he permitted rolled-up sleeves. The news of this went like wildfire down to the lowest private in the Corps. It marked a basic difference between Patton and him and established Bradley forever after as the 'soldier's soldier' who looked out for the little guy. Certainly he made the going through that jungle a bit easier for all of us.

Captain C. P. "Pete" Brownley, 9th Reconnaissance Troop, was on special duty as a liaison officer to II Corps, and recollects the General and his headquarters:

I spent most of my time being briefed at Division and travelling to II Corps with that information. There I would attend daily briefings and hit the road back to the 9th with information and orders. It was intensely interesting to be associated with making the 'big picture.' The mess was good, always served on tables, three times a day. Corps was in a building rather than in tents.

My major impression of General Bradley was that of about all the reporters. He was quiet, unassuming, unruffled but unquestionably in command. He was the antithesis of his predecessor in every way. For example, compared with Patton's big entourage tying up traffic for miles when he passed, I can recall coming across Bradley parked at the side of the road waiting patiently for a supply convoy to move through.

For most men of the 9th Northern Tunisia was where they had their first contact with the combat soldiers of Allied forces. They were struck by the Europeans' class consciousness as well as by their casual attitudes toward war, and their general abilitiy to make do with relatively less in the way of supporting gear.

Captain Alex T. Forrest, operations officer of the 15th Engineer Battalion, was part of the 9th's advance party to the British and recollects:

At the conclusion of El Guettar, Captain Ed Kuklewicz, the S2, and I were ordered to the town of Djebel Abiod to coordinate the transfer of materials from the 46th Division's Royal Engineers. Upon arrival and after a late dinner, Ed and I walked back to our vehicles, laid out our bed rolls and prepared to go to sleep. We had passed by and had a word with our drivers who were sitting around a fire exchanging food and talk with British enlisted men. They were still within earshot and just before nodding off I heard one say, 'Oy say, mite, was that the bloody Captain?' He was surprised that we had taken care of ourselves. British officers had batmen.

Captain George A. Pedrick, S1 of the lst Battalion, 39th Infantry, remembers:

The British were in a holding position at the time and there wasn't much action. They were courteous and reserved as expected, also they were experienced and relaxed. They were hospitable with their five-gallon tins which held a mixture of powdered milk, sugar and tea leaves ground very fine; a couple of spoons full of that mix in a cup of hot water and you had a great cup of tea. While they were helpful I had the feeling that they thought we had a lot to learn about fighting the Germans.

Major H. W. Lange, 84th Field Artillery Battalion S3, remembers:

Soon after we arrived and went into position in the Sedjenane area I went for a walk on the nearby road. It was quiet and, as the vegetation by the road was very thick, I seemed quite alone even though our positions were not far away. Then, along came a British command car with five passengers. I noticed their dressy appearance--no helmets. The fellow in the place of honor wore a red cap so, when the car stopped, I saluted him.

He asked: 'Have you seen a gun sight on this road?'

I thought to myself, how strange. Why would this big shot have to go looking for a lost gun sight? But I told him that I had been walking back and forth for the past thirty minutes and keeping an eye peeled for mines and scorpions but had seen nothing unusual.

His nibs looked at me curiously and then told his driver to push on. It occurred to me later that we had a translation difficulty. The Brits must have been looking for gun positions, possibly ours, a 'gun site' by their terminology.

Captain W. Joseph Hanks, 9th Divarty S2, recalls of the British:

We always regarded the British as being very methodical. While being escorted around one of their artillery positions the English officer was telling us about the Boche habit of shelling the mess line every day at noon. 'Well,' he said, 'we fixed that. We changed the eating time to 11 A.M. and, you know, those methodical Germans still shell the area at 12 every day.'

I can still recall how grateful I was when this 'leftenant' offered me some of his 'compote' that morning at breakfast. 'Man,' I thought, 'that's the best stuff I've ever tasted.' At that time we had only been overseas six months but our families never sent anything like that.

Once the British were out of there, rations went back to the accustomed American C variety which could be eaten cold but only if one had to. Pfc. Trevor Jones recalls that, if one was near a vehicle, heating a C was simply a matter of setting it on the engine's manifold but the technique had tragic consequences for their 2nd Platoon jeep driver, Ellis Jones:

One day Jones, with Russell Stover and Richard Lostasso as passengers, was making tracks back down the main road through the Sedjenane valley. During daylight that area was under observation by the bad guys so one hustled. The road wasn't much to begin with and a couple of battles back and forth over it hadn't helped. Jone's passengers were getting a rough ride down the straightaway but when they came to the curve it was all over. The jeep hit a tree head on. Jones and Stover were killed and Lostasso was severely injured. Inspection of the jeep showed that a can of Cs had slid off the manifold and wedged the steering post so that it wouldn't turn. What a price to pay for the simple pleasure of eating a warm C-ration.

In anticipation of the difficulty of supply and evacuation in the hilly, essentially roadless sector assigned the 9th Division, 300 mules were obtained from the French military and allocated to the infantry regiments. Sometimes French Army harness was available but more often native improvisations of rope had to do. Regimental S4's generally suballocated the beasts to Battalion S4s, along with the problem of learning how to employ them. By this time, mule-packing was practically a lost military skill but, fortunately, there were enough farm-bred soldiers around who knew about the care and handling of mules. The experiences of the Division's many "drugstore cowboys" made some lasting impressions.

2nd Lieutenant Don W. Erion, S4, 2nd Battalion, 60th Infantry, for example, has this opinion:

> *Trying to keep the front lines supplied in the hills and wadis of Northern Tunisia was a nightmare. Our attempt to use mules was a disaster as we had no mule skinners. Many times we found that carrying as much as we could on our backs was the most effective way to go.*

On the other hand Pfc. Charles T. Walker, D Company, 60th Infantry was grateful for the beasts:

> *We were moving in a wide, flanking maneuver around Green and Bald Hills over extremely difficult terrain. Fortunately we acquired some burros to help carry the 81mm mortar ammo. The man in charge said that two shoulder packs on each burro would be okay, one across the shoulders and the other over its hips. But the packs were too long and chafed the sides of the burro's legs. I was assigned to lead one but after about six hours my burro quit. I tried to adjust the packs but it didn't work. So I carried one of the packs. He liked that. The next day he looked so pitiful I decided to carry both packs and pull the burro. He didn't like this either so we went back to sharing the load.*

Those more experienced had better luck as 1st Lieutenant Charles Scheffel, A Company, 39th Infantry, tried to demonstrate:

> *As the Company was getting low on supplies I volunteered to go back to the Battalion command post (CP) and get more. When I got there the S4 Section already had about 20 mules loaded with water cans, field rations and ammunition. Each was to be led by a soldier from Headquarters Company. I would take the lead mule.*
>
> *It wasn't as easy as I had thought. It was now dark and there was no way I could head back the way I had come. The mules seemed determined to follow existing paths so at first I simply tried to steer them to those which seemed to lead back to the positions. None of these paths, however, led up to the high ground and low ground made me nervous. When I concluded that we might have come too far, I called a halt. There was no sense in feeding the Germans.*
>
> *By now there was a misty rain falling. All the men were get-*

ting wet but the mules with their loads were sweaty and stayed warm. I remembered something from my days back on the farm in Oklahoma. I grabbed my mule's two front legs in my right hand and the rear pair in my left. With a hard jerk he dropped, water cans clanking, and I jumped on top to hold him down. It worked. He laid still and I snuggled down between his legs next to his belly. The man in back must have thought I'd gone crazy and my example stopped there. The rest stayed up and cold all night. When it got light we weren't far from home and the troops were glad to have the stuff.

60th Infantry pack train, 26 April 1943.
(Army Signal Corps photo.)

lst Lieutenant Harold W. Smith, commander of L Company, 60th Infantry, recollects:

> *We had pack mules but no food for them. I saw them break cactus down with their hooves to get at the pulp. They didn't understand commands given in English and few of the GIs had been mule skinners, but there must have been a meeting of the minds. We managed to get rations by this means. We didn't starve but I don't think anyone gained weight either.*

Pfc. Trevor Jones, 9th Quartermaster Company, was a truck driver who was "retreaded" in the closing days of the battle. He remembers:

> *I became part of the mule-skinning brigade hauling rations and ammo forward to the troops. Those mules were probably nasty and stubborn under normal conditions. With our inexperience and ineptness, along with the occasional shelling that came our way, they were almost impossible to handle.*
>
> *My only prior experience with this sort of thing was at the local park's pony ride back in Scranton, but gradually I learned how to tie granny knots and load the pack saddles. Then we would set out, sometimes on trails, often through the brush and thorns, over the hills and down the wadis. Eventually we'd arrive at some point occupied by 60th guys or their Goum friends. We'd rest and then head back, sometimes packing litters with the wounded.*

2nd Lieutenant Fred R. Veno was a replacement officer to Headquarters Company, lst Battalion, 47th Infantry. He recalls:

> *I was new and still 'spare parts' when we took up positions facing Green Hill. Not long after this we were issued a small herd of mules, complete with pack saddles. The farm boys among our GIs greeted them with open arms and showed the city lads how to take care of them. The mules did a very good job and we would have been lost without them.*

Again Captain Alex T. Forrest of the 15th Engineer Battalion:

> *Although it is to be aknowledged that the roads we built and maintained played an important part in the battle, one must not overlook the contribution of the mule trains in the initial supply of the troops. I well-remember a cold, wet night when I was at a control point we had established by the by-pass bridge built over the Oued Doumiss. To guide traffic at night, 'Christmas lights' (perforated cans with gasoline-soaked dirt inside), had been*

placed to show the way off and back onto the main road. Suddenly, out of the blackness came a plaintiff Southern voice, 'Cap'n can y'all tell me where the 47th Infantry is at?' After my instructing him, the soldier disappeared into the darkness with his half-dozen mules. About two hours later, out of the darkness again came the same voice with the same query. Either my directions had been poor or the 47th had moved out.

Another change and improvement in Northern Tunisia were better maps and more copies of them. And there was the diminished capacity of the Luftwaffe. While Messerschmitt 109s were still about, swooping in to strafe the main road, this came to be less and less frequent. Soldiers could see that the Army Air Corps was supporting their exertions and this had a positive effect on morale.

Since Northern Tunisia's rough terrain and heavy vegetation limited even foot mobility, it increased the significance of low-level decision making. What remained useful from the company officers' prior experience at El Guettar or Maknassy was an appreciation of the German's tactical skill, the importance of the high ground and how to use supporting fires to get on it. Good small unit leadership was even more critical to the 9th's success up north because the going was extremely arduous and opportunities for weaker soldiers to get lost and "goof off" were more plentiful. As never before, by maintaining unit cohesion, platoon leaders and their NCOs would determine the outcome of the fighting in Northern Tunisia.

General Eddy alluded to these points in his letter to all members of the Division distributed on April 22, 1943:

This Division will shortly be called upon to take part in the combined attack of the 18th Army Group that will mark the end of Axis resistance in North Africa.

In your previous engagements at Port Lyautey, Safi and in Southern Tunisia you have done well.[2] You have endured the privations of campaign, suffered heavy casualties, and have emerged from your baptism of fire with the stamp of approval given only through battlefield experience.

We are now to have the opportunity of attacking alongside our comrades of the 2nd U.S. Corps, the British 1st and 8th Armies, and the French 19th Corps and Corps Franc d'Afrique. We are making history. I charge you and expect you to put forth every ounce of effort with a ruthlessness that has been taught us by our enemies. This I know you will do. We must advance and keep driving forward no matter how hard the going may be. Resistance met must be reduced by outflanking maneuvers by all units from the platoon up.

A world spotlight will be focused upon us from the moment we attack until we have killed, captured or driven every Axis soldier from Tunisia. We have the finest arms and equipment in the world. We outnumber our opponents both on land and in the air. The cards are stacked in our favor. Anything less than annihilation of the enemy will be a blot on our record.

I have the utmost confidence in the Division. I know that every officer and man will put into the coming fight everything he has in him so that our Division will contribute its full share towards a speedy, decisive victory. Good luck.

Notes

1. A. J. Liebling, *Quest for Mollie & Other War Pieces,* p. 263.

2. Henry Thomas J., "The Avenging Ghosts of the 9th," *Saturday Evening Post,* (6 July 1946), page 24.

3. General Eddy's omission of the 39th Infantry's accomplishment at Algiers is noteworthy and suggests a Freudian slip due to his animus towards the regiment's commander, Colonel Brown, which would soon come to a head. The general had no cause to slight the performance of the 39th in the November 8th landing at Algiers or in the Battle of El Guettar.

ARTILLERY SUPPORT

Brigadier General "Red" Irwin was not his usual cheerful 50-year-old self at breakfast. He had been stewing much of the night about the profound artillery problems caused by the Division's 28-mile front. It took almost that much acreage to find decent positions for his own four battalions of howitzers and the two battalions plus one battery of attached artillery. They had not only to cover the wide frontage but also to be able to mass fires in order to overwhelm enemy positions or countermeasures that developed. It was a big order and the incessant flies weren't making the damp foggy morning any more pleasant.

The 9th's artillery commander was not the kind to think much about it but everyone knew he was under the gun. It was not official yet but the redleg grapevine had it that Irwin's second star and command of an infantry division were in the works. The tall and genial West Pointer had no doubts about his ability to handle the multi-branch character of that next assignment. After all, he originally had been a horse cavalryman and served in that capacity with Pershing and Patton chasing Pancho Villa into Mexico. The artillery business came later because, as he put it to friends, gunnery problems were more intellectually challenging than figuring the right proportions of hay and oats to feed horses. But the general's immediate problems of supporting the 9th's attack in Northern Tunisia had priority among his cares now. Beyond this, it was always tough living up to a reputation made so early in the game.

9th Division Artillery had been practically the only part of the division able to respond to cries for help that came back from II U.S. Corps when Rommel unleashed his Afrika Korps at Faid Pass and Gafsa earlier in the year.[1] The bulk of the division had been slowly making its way eastward from Morocco when the tocsin sounded. Division Artillery and the cannon companies of the 47th and 60th Regiments, being mobile, were rushed ahead and in 100 hours completed a 777-mile forced march near Thala in Tunisia, in time on February 22nd to help meager British forces hold back a wing of Rommel's attack.

Irwin's force had gone into position in the dark with poor maps and a murky picture of the immediate tactical situation. It was a shock in the morning to find the command post and the light battalions on a forward slope, naked of defilade, with the 10th Panzer Division tanks moving towards them. In the end the artillerymen were bore-sighting those tanks while swarms of Stuka divebombers screamed down on them. Then, Rommel, frustrated by his other wing's inability to grab the Allied supply base at Tebessa, and the unwillingness of his counterpart in Northern Tunisia to contribute fully to the effort, suddenly broke off the offensive. On the Allied side, the nick-of-time arrival of Brigadier General S. Leroy Irwin's task force and its frontline heroism in the face of heavy odds were the only bright spots in an otherwise dismal battle. The 9th's artillerymen and infantry cannoneers received the Distinguished Unit Citation, the division's first such recognition of its units.

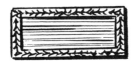

After Major General George Patton took over and reenergized II Corps, its elements were thrown into offensives at El Guettar and Maknassy in Southern Tunisia and 9th Division Artillery resumed its normal role of supporting infantry attacks at both places. Again the superiority of German air power limited Patton's success but the action provided the infantry-artillery teams of the 9th further opportunities to work out organization and communication problems. After the 9th moved north it was fighting for the first time as a complete division and its major elements, the infantry regiments with their supporting artillery battalions, had been honed to a keen edge.

Ninth Division Artillery was good, so concern for possible failure was not causing Irwin's loss of sleep. He genuinely felt for the division's infantry who had to carry the ball, and he wanted them to have the full measure of the artillery's incomparable support. Irwin was a team player as well as a man of many varied interests. An accomplished watercolorist who was intensely interested in all forms of art, he was equally fascinated with science and the skills of engineering. He was gregarious, interested in the thoughts of others and skilled at drawing them out. Enlisted men and junior officers were made to feel significant and they responded with extra devotion to their jobs. The general knew that they would do well in the coming battle. He just wished there weren't so many imponderables at this stage. Like all good forward observers, he wanted to see forever.

The general was joined at the table under the mess tent by Colonel Douglas J. Page, his executive officer. Page was another graduate of the U. S. Military Academy, class of 1916, a year behind Irwin. The colonel had taken an advance party to reconnoiter the artillery situation in the Sedjenane valley even before the El Guettar battle began. Together, Irwin and Page planned the stealthy takeover from the British so as not to alert the enemy of the change. That part was relatively easy. The difficulty lay in planning ahead.

The wide frontage, few roads and limitations on cross country mobility meant that Division Artillery would not be able to mass all of its available firepower at any point on the front. The "Serenade," or "Time on Target (TOT)," as this technique was dubbed, had great shocking power and was frequently desirable in either defensive or offensive situations. The problem in the Sedjenane was overcome in part by attachment of additional artillery units to the 9th. These included the 62nd Armored Field Artillery Battalion (105mm self-propelled howitzers), the 185th Field Artillery Battalion (155mm howitzers) and a battery of the 36th Field Artillery (155mm guns). A battery of the 62nd was placed in direct support of the Corps Franc d'Afrique. The 155mm guns were especially useful for counterbattery purposes.

Initially, Irwin and Page had thought it might be necessary to split the heavier general support artillery into two groups to cover the front. It was finally decided, however, to retain centralized control since the communications system that was improvised could support this arrangement.

'How are the eggs, General?' Page asked.

'I've let them get cold, Doug, while wondering how we're going to cover the reverse slopes of these hills with the wide frontage, few roads and the jungle. We've got the space but we've got

to cut our way into every position with machetes,' Irwin groused.

Page observed: 'But it's fortunate that the enemy is thinned out. If this attack unfolds like I think it will, we'll only be meeting him in strength at a few critical points. We can predict where these will be. We're not going to have to chase him all around the ball park and we'll have time to get set for a change. It's not like before.'

'Hell, Doug, aren't you the rosie Miss Sunshine this morning,' the general beamed. 'Why don't you bottle that stuff and send some up to division. Those guys have more to worry about than we do. They haven't got a camouflage net big enough to cover that villa they're in and the Luftwaffe's going to have a field day with 'em.'

The colonel chuckled: 'And did you get a load of those military policemen (MPs) dressed as Arabs out on the road? Who does the G2 think he's kidding? Half of those real Arabs passing by have Leica cameras under their bathrobes and are drawing their pay in Reichmarks.'

Both officers laughed so loudly that heads were raised and faces broke into smiles in the now-filled mess tent. lst Lieutenant Bert Waller, the communications officer, approached and saluted Irwin and Page:

'I have a report on how we're making out in getting the communications up and running with the battalions, General. Do you have time now?'

Irwin responded: 'Of course, Waller. It looks like you've been up all night--just like Thala and El Guettar, eh?'

Waller smiled and said: 'No sir, but most of the night. We have almost completed setting up the North and South switches to get ready for a split-command post if you need it. It's pretty rough out there on those skinny roads with the heavy traffic. Sometimes, we're laying cross country over rough ground when we don't know where all the mines are. Over the long stretches we are using captured German boosters which work better than ours do, even when we get enough of them from Signal. We have. . .'

Page broke in: 'What about radio. Do you need my command car?'

Waller told him that he had already used the general's car with the SCR-608 dual receiver radio as a relay between the main Division Artillery CP and the battalions, but requested a rain-check on Page's vehicle in case he needed another. As it turned out, Page's frequency modulated set was used to avoid terrain which interferred with "line-of-sight" communications. Radio relay was also used effectively to connect directly the 9th's forward observers with the "Long Toms" when they had targets that were out of range of their own units.

Irwin and Page then went next door to the Fire Direction Center (FDC) where Captain Bruce January, Division Artillery Headquarters Battery CO, reported that meteorological data had been obtained and distributed. Major Evert E. Stong, S3, and Captain W. Joseph Hanks, S2, then briefed the general on the situation. They were assisted by Sergeant Nick DeMella, and Corporals Tony Loscalzos and Ed Marks. Stong first reported on the move from southern Tunisia. The battalions had moved and gone into their new posiitons without incident. They were ready to fire. The log of the 34th Field Artillery Battalion shows that it wasn't as easy as the S3 suggested:[2]

> *The Battalion S3 (Major Neil Cox) ordered fire direction personnel to install the 'night command post' (blackout tent) for immediate use. The battalion command post was situated in a rock bed adjacent to mine tracks. The fire direction personnel, confronted with the task of digging through rock for slit trenches, were told by Captain Lucas, Assistant S3, that they could pile up rocks around the area the length of a slit trench but to be extremely careful not to have any loose rocks upon building the structure. Lt. Colonel Westmoreland again reminded the Operations Sergeant, Message Center Chief and S2 Clerk of the battalion standard policy requiring them to keep a container, quart-size, filled with gasoline, with the intent of destroying all information which in any way may be helpful to the enemy.*

Stong continued with his briefing, reviewing the fire plan:

> '*General, overlays have gone to the battalions showing the fire plans we wish them to follow. Night harassing fires are scheduled. All battalions are set to fire Corps' "Serenades or TOTs" when we give the word. The S3s have been reminded of the following three special standard operating procedures (SOP) items we wish followed in this operation:*
>
> '*First, at any time one of our bombing missions materializes, all battalions within range are to drop a concentration on the bombed area immediately.*
>
> '*The second item is that any time an observer can see an enemy gun itself, and not just the flash, the whole battery area is to be neutralized. After that, precision adjustment can be made to destroy each visible piece.*

*'Third, as at El Guettar, we want each direct support
battalion to be ready at any time to survey in the infantry frontline positions using flares, and to mark objectives with smoke on
call of the infantry commanders.'*

Hanks reported that the German artillery in the 9th Division's
sector for the moment consisted of two batteries of 105 mm howitzers,
one of 150mm howitzers and two 170mm guns. The enemy had, in
addition, eight self-propelled 75mm howitzers and up to 10 mobile
88mm guns. Of the latter, all but two which were now facing the
CFA, were in the southern part of the corps sector but these could
displace rapidly to positions facing the 9th. German tanks also had
been employed as artillery but not effectivly thus far due to an apparent shortage of high-explosive ammunition.

The S2 also covered the dispositions made of the attached 434th
Coast Artillery Battalion (AA), Battery H, 67th Coast Artillery (AA)
and the 894th Tank Destroyer Battalion which was providing close-in
ground protection for their installations.

Stong then returned to cover the ammunition situation. Corps
had established dumps at Djebel Abiod (three days supply) and at
Tamara Station (one day). It had prescribed 100 rounds per gun on
site for 105s and 70 rounds per 155 and Stong believed that amount
inadequate. General Irwin recalled the dire ammunition situation they
had experienced at Thala and directed:

*'Evert, I want each 105 to have at least 150 rounds on site
and Westy's 155s to have 100 rounds. If they can carry more,
do it. Same applies to attached Corps units. Doug, give "Hooks"
Howell at Corps a call and let him know what we are doing.'*

The briefing completed, General Irwin departed for the observation post (OP). Major Stong recalls:

*About this time the CP was raided by enemy air. All headed
for cover as the planes strafed; that is, all but a British major
who was on liaison duty with us. He just stood there calmly with
hands in his pockets and remarked, 'Hell, I've been at this for
four years away from home. I'm not the least concerned about
getting hit. This one's not for me.' Sure enough, it was not.*

And not far away, lst Lieutenant Louis M. Prince, executive officer of Battery B, 60th Field Artillery Battalion, was scribbling some
observations in his notebook. Prince knew about the ban on keeping
diaries but did not figure he was violating it because he did not write
every day, and his entries were mixed with a lot of other battery business. His entries catch the flavor of those hours before the Sedjenane

battle began:

Tuesday, April 20th, 1943: *Here we are in our fifth battle and it is by far the most pleasant. We are east of Sedjenane and about 30 miles west of Bizerte. We are supposed to be holding the northernmost part of the circle in which the Germans are now penned. From our OPs we can see them and from theirs they can see us but no one does any shooting which makes it very nice. Yesterday they shelled one of the batteries of the 84th with 88s and there has been considerable air activity but on the whole it's a lovely battle (so far.)*

Sedjenane, like Maknassy, has been in German and Allied hands a number of times, so the road up here is a terrible mess but part of the ride, the part we made in daytime, was perfectly beautiful. We were on a very high mountain road overlooking the Mediterranean. Beautiful beaches and charming French villages all along the road, with vineyards and small farms up the mountain side. What a shame to have war in such a beautiful country! The weather, too, is lovely which is very unusual for us when we are in battle.

Sedjenane has 1,000-pound bomb craters in it, 12 feet deep.

I suppose we'll stay like this a day or two more, and then probably make an attack. It's the first time the 9th Division has fought as a unit (almost every regiment and battalion in it has been in battle, but was attached to some other unit.) Like at Mehdia, we were alone with the 60th Infantry, 70th Tank, 15th Engineer, 540th Engineer, etc. At Thala it was the 9th Division Artillery attached to one of the British First Army corps. At Sened and Maknassy we were attached to the 1st Armored Division. I hope the 9th Division does all right. I guess the 60th and maybe the 84th have been in the most battles. It certainly has been enough for me. Incidentally, the prospects of my being transferred and sent back to the United States are still not dark. General Irwin, I believe, is compiling a list of officers eligible for promotion who have been overseas for six months.

I would be perfectly willing to leave, I believe. I would miss B Battery, but not so much as I miss Betty! So here's hoping that after this campaign I am again subjected to the U-boat menace!

We know now that Sousse has fallen and belongs to the Eighth Army. The Axis has only Bizerte and Tunis and they are surrounded on all sides.

Lieutenant Welsh is back with us again to take Jim's place (he will probably not be back.) I'm so glad he's here. He is so entertaining. Also we have a new lieutenant (only 20 years old. I used to think I was so young!) I thought it was hard to come to a battery in the middle of maneuvers but he came in the middle of a battle!

B Battery, 60th FA in action, 27 April 1943.
(From the collection of Louis M. Prince, Cincinnati, OH.)

A few days later, Prince continued:

> <u>*Thursday, April 22nd, 1943:*</u> *In position 10 miles northeast of Sedjenane (about three miles south of the Mediterranean near Cap Serrat) and 30 or 35 miles west of Bizerte. Tomorrow morning at H-hour we start an attack supporting the 60th Infantry. We are making a flanking movement toward the east, to a crossroad about 15 miles away where we will meet the 39th and 47th Infantry who are going down the main road. It will take us about five or six days if it's successful. There are also three battalions of French Moroccan troops and one battalion of Algerian 'ear cutters' near but they won't have any part of the attack.*
>
> *The British First Army, now on our right, and the Eighth Army have already started their attacks. It seems to me as if we had been put in here as an accomodation because the British wanted to finish this up alone, but General Patton wouldn't hear of it. He wanted to be 'in on the kill.' They are trying to split Tunis and Bizerte.*
>
> *Once we get beyond these awful mountains it will be much easier. Tanks can't even operate in these hills so the 1st Armored Division is in reserve, as is the 34th. The 1st Division is attacking on our right.*
>
> *So far in this battle things have been very quiet. Lots of airplanes but no air attacks and some artillery fire but not on us. I imagine the fireworks will really start again tomorrow.*
>
> *Saw Bill Mauser of the 84th yesterday and others from Fort Sill and Fort Bragg in the 84th. He had as bad a time at El Guettar as we did at Maknassy. He got a direct hit on a gun and foxhole which was apparently as gruesome as our howitzer blowing up. Whoever is reading this, if anyone does besides me, can be glad I have't put in any of the gruesome, bloody details, but I won't ever forget them.*

lst Lieutenant William W. Clarke, survey officer of 9th Division Artillery, recalls:

> *I spent most of my time in Northern Tunisia trying to establish a flash base, or trying to tie-in the attached 155mm rifles. We never did get the former job done so that we could fire counterbattery at night. The consensus among the senior artillery officers was that trying to locate enemy guns by this means was like trying to zero-in on summer sheet lightning.*
>
> *It was scarey work because we were somewhere out in front on black nights without much of an idea of where we were. One night we spent most of the time walking about a well-mined field.*

The 'Long Toms' were another great frustration. They were down in a wadi where we couldn't get control to the gun position. That is, having their exact positions plotted without traversing for days, and the only triangulation locations were inside enemy positions. In spite of not being an exceptionally bright mathematician, I worked out a solution for solving the triangle when the base could not be occupied. When the pressure's on you can surprise yourself. The technique developed also required that you take a true azimuth by a sun observation. I didn't have a clue on that one but, fortunately, the instrument sergeant had been trained to do this by Captain Bill Hanks, the S2. I can't remember the Sergeant's name but he came from the West Virginia coal mines with less than an elementary school education. Under Hanks he had mastered practical trigonometry and planned to run for county surveyor after the war. He was killed in Normandy.

Although they had been around for some time, the light aircraft of 9th Division Artillery were used tactically for the first time in Northern Tunisia. Over 100 missions were flown covering not only observation of enemy positions and targets of opportunity, but communications, photography and administration. The history of the 34th Field Artillery Battalion describes an early aviation mission of that unit:[2]

At 1445 (May 1) Lt. Col. Westmoreland ordered Lieutenant Bowen to be prepared to observe base point and Green Hill in a plane allotted to battalion. Lieutenant Bowen was also ordered to pick up Lieutenant Gauthier (observer) at Headquarters Battery. At 1600, Lieutenant Bowen landed on an adjacent field and picked up Lieutenant Gauthier. They immediately took off and at 1630 (were) flying over battalion position area, communicating with battalion command post by radio. After observing rounds of fire on Green Hill, Lieutenant Bowen returned with Piper Cub to rear echelon.

lst Lieutenant William C. Bowen, Jr., recalls:

Control of the planes was decentralized initially. It was not until Sicily that we centralized all Division Artillery aircraft, normally ten planes. Most of our early flights were for communications, column control, camouflage checks and administrative purposes. It really came into its own as a primary means of observation in Normandy where the hedgerows hampered ground observation.

Captain W. Joseph Hanks, 9th Division Artillery S2:

> *The Division Artillery Air OP Section (two planes) came under my staff supervision. We had a Captain Garner and Lieutenants Tommy Hall and Severson. They were all good and quickly improved. This was the first time we dared use them because of the Boche air superiority. Everyone looked after the pilots when they were up. The minute a German plane was heard the ground OP crews would alert the cub pilots who would hit the deck and stay until 'All Clear.'*
>
> *I took a ride in the Sedjenane valley. Captain Garner looked back and saw me hanging onto the overhead braces. He laughed and reminded me that if the plane went down, so would the braces.*

Major H. W. Lange, 84th Field Artillery Battalion S3, remembers:

> *In the absence of good maps in Africa, we frequently had to make our own with blank grid sheets, plotting whatever few road junction coordinates and other locations we achieved. We also fired 'check concentrations' on key terrain points which forward observers might later see or reach. It was then easy to shift from these to developing targets of opportunity. Often the need for secrecy prevented pre-assault shooting so the vital 'base point registration' could only be done at the minute of attack. This is where the Cub aircraft was important in that it allowed the precise location of the very first rounds.*

Pfc. Leo Feinstein, B Battery, 60th Field Artillery Battalion, recalls:

> *We were having air attacks at this time and when they came we would race to man the .50 caliber machine guns mounted on the trucks. We never seemed to hit anything and the German pilots became cocky, flying lower and lower as they bombed and strafed us. One of our guys finally managed to hit the bomb being carried under the belly of a Stuka dive bomber. It blew up and pieces of the plane came floating down. Even though the raid continued, everybody got up off the ground and cheered like at a ball game. The Jerrys flew much higher after that.*

Division Artillery unit logs and journals include other highpoints of the operation in Northern Tunisia. Writing of its new positions in the Sedjenane valley, an historian of Lt. Colonel Justin "Doc" Stoll's 84th Field Artillery Battalion wrote:[3]

> *The area was covered by a dense scrub from 3 to 6 feet high and good camouflage was possible. Constant check had to be*

made on this camouflage as this was the first available cover since we entered Tunisia and everyone had grown lax.

The 84th had trouble with Germans in the air and on the ground:

Two Messerschmitt 109s strafed the road in the battalion's vicinity and bombed Sedjenane. About 1350, 200 Germans were observed moving forward and were brought under fire by A Battery's observer. They dispersed and vanished into a draw. At 1500 they were sighted again in the act of setting up mortars and trying to capture the high ground the observer was occupying. They were fired on again with excellent results. Notified the 47th Infantry commander of the situation and troops were soon sent to reinforce the area. At 1830, eight German planes flew over our position and bombed Sedjenane.

On 27 April, Lt. Colonel Clinton L. Adams' 60th Field Artillery Battalion found:[4]

The need for long-range counterbattery weapons was felt heavily. The German batteries, confident in their knowledge of our 12,200 yard range, would move just out of our range and use their greater range to bring us under fire. The battalion obtained the support of two 155mm rifles, then gave the Germans a very thorough shellacking as they were slow to believe they were outranged.

Lt. Colonel James T. "Bull" Dawson's 26th Field Artillery Battalion had a big day on April 30th.[5] It helped the 39th Infantry seize Hill 406 which uncovered many German installations. The forward observers, Lieutenants Bryant, Flowers, Ledbetter, Mynatt and White, had a "turkey shoot." The Battalion fired 4,497 rounds that day. Private John Clouser, a member of the 26th's fire direction center, recalls:

Colonel Dawson was popularly known as 'Bull' from the cartoon character he resembled. He was proud of our rate of fire, which caused German prisoners to want to see the American's 'automatic artillery,' until he was reprimanded by General Irwin for overheating his barrels.

Again, Major H. W. Lange, S3 of the 84th, recalls:

General Eisenhower, writing in Crusade in Europe, *cites the effectiveness of our artillery as one of the reasons for the Tunisian victory. We had a very high rate of fire because we mostly used fixed ammunition and could load and fire much faster than the enemy or our allies. Also we had excellent communications and rapid fire direction.*

1st Lieutenant Bert C. Waller, Division Artillery's communications officer, concludes:

> *The estimate of the opposing artillery was correct and they were hammered unmercifully. The fire plan was implemented with no great difficulty, notwithstanding the wide frontage and other difficulties encountered. The infantry became sold on 'leaning into supporting artillery fire.'*
>
> *Because of heavy fire needs, frequent position changes, mined roads and difficulty of night supply, the battalions found it necessary to carry an even greater ammunition stock than General Irwin specified. For example, the 60th Field Artillery Battalion carried an average of 4,000 rounds, over 300 rounds per weapon, on position. Between April 19th and May 9th, the 60th moved seven times and fired 12,785 rounds. Altogether, Division Artillery, including attached units, fired 40,576 rounds.*
>
> *In the Sedjenane, 9th Division Artillery displayed a high level of operational flexibility. A 'grid' communications system was adopted which permitted maximum alternate routing of traffic. Units established communications from supporting to supported, superior to subordinate and laterally. This enabled the rapid shifting of assignments from direct to general support or reinforcing. Battalions fired missions with precision, not only in their own sectors but in others as well. Massed fires were highly effective.*
>
> *The artillery was first-rate but it only did its job, as it had been trained to do, with good people and outstanding leadership. Now, after three major battles, we had learned a great deal about combat and how it should function as a part of the division team.*

Notes

1. The 39th Infantry's Cannon and Anti-tank Companies, and its 3rd Battalion were already in Tunisia and attached to the 1st Armored Division at this time. They were caught up in the maelstrom of Rommel's offensive, suffered heavy casualties and lost most of their heavy weapons.

2. *Historical Records and History of 34th Field Artillery Battalion, U.S. Army, 10 June 1943,* pp. 24 & 37.

3. *History of 84th Field Artillery Battalion for Year 1943, 4 May 1943,* p. 13.

4. *History of 60th Field Artillery Battalion for Year 1943,* 11 January 1945, pp. 1-2.

5. *Narrative of the 26th Field Artillery Battalion in the Battle of the Sedjenane and Mateur, 13 May 1943,* p. 3.

MORE BATTLE PREPARATIONS

Some members of the 9th were in the Sedjenane valley even before the fighting at Maknassy and El Guettar began. Major Frederick C. Feil, the 47th's executive officer, was in charge of the party which sat down with representatives of the British 46th Infantry Division to work out the 9th's take-over of that unit's sector. The 46th, commanded by Major General H. A. Freeman-Atwood, then consisted of the 138th Infantry and the lst Parachute Brigades. British units were somewhat smaller than their Yank counterparts. Feil recollects that one of Freeman-Atwood's early orders concerning the relief was that his units would determine how many foxholes the Americans would require and to dig them before they showed up. Another in the 9th's group, Captain Dean T. Vanderhoef, Assistant G2, recalls that a British lieutenant colonel was assigned as intelligence liaison. There was no holding back on information concerning the enemy whose situation at the time was as fluid as that of the Allies. German units too were being shifted widely as the front contracted.

General Eddy's division would be facing the main body of the German's Division von Manteuffel. Its 962nd Infantry Regiment defended a sector from the coast to the hills south of the Sedjenane river valley with four battalions. Next to it the 160th Panzer Grenadier Regiment held a nine-mile zone with another three battalions. Von Manteuffel's third regiment, named for its commander Barenthin, was still further south opposite the lst U.S.Infantry Division. In the hills which the 9th had to win, therefore, were initially seven enemy infantry battalions. On April 27-28 some Italian units and two German reconnaissance battalions would raise the total to nine battalion-size units, about 5,000 men. [1]

The relief would be gradual and incremental. The 47th Infantry was to take over the positions of the 138th Brigade on the night of April 12-13 and the 39th would relieve the parachutists three nights later. As part of the plan to deceive the Germans, the 60th would be held back in a concealed position near the town of Djebel Abiod until April 19th. Then it would come forward by night in stages to reach its assault position at H-hour on the 23rd. In the meantime the artillery, reconnaissance, engineer and finally signal units would switch places. The deliberate character of the relief was meant to preserve secrecy of the forthcoming attack; incidentally, it provided most of the Americans their first contact with the British fighting man and an opportunity to learn something of his casual ways.

lst Lieutenant Chester Braune, Jr., aide to the 9th's assistant division commander, recalls:

The valley through which the road to Bizerete ran was flat and controlled by the Germans from Green and Bald Hills. The British had made a couple of 'Light Brigade' charges with light vehicles into the mouths of the Kraut 88s and the place was littered with burnt out vehicles.

After talking to the British and looking things over, General Stroh asked me what I would do with the 9th. I said: 'General, I'd put one regiment on line and flank with the other, keeping one in reserve.' I had learned that in ROTC.

The general said: 'That's fine, but we need one regiment on line and it must make big enough waves so that we can flank with two regiments.' He then had me color the contours on his map so that he could pick out the highest ground at a glance and plan the routes of advance and successive objectives for the attacking regiments.

Outside the town of Sedjenane the command post was in a two-story villa and we went to some lengths to maintain its innocence. MPs stationed out on the road were dressed as Arabs. No one was allowed to use the front door. We went around to the back and climbed a ladder to a second-story window. Despite this, we were strafed by an Messerschmitt l09 one day. It blew a large hole in the roof and scattered tiles around.

lst Lieutenant Robert E. Hulslander, I Company, 47th Infantry, remembers about the advance party:

While getting the lay of the land where I Company was to go from the Brits and having a fine cup of tea, the Germans shelled. No one was hurt and it was taken rather matter-of-factly. The relief came off after dark without incident. The next day we saw more of the Germans when their planes came low down the highway to Jefna strafing everything that moved.

Not everything about the relief went smoothly. 2nd Lieutenant Raymond J. Brugger, K Company, 39th Infantry, remembers:

Beyond the town on Sedjenane we took up positions on top of a hill across the valley from our regimental headquarters. We relieved a detachment of British paratroopers who left us an officer presumably familiar with the terrain and trails. Under his guidance we put out a listening post which later turned out to be on the wrong path. Certain outposts put out on forward hills turned out to be fiascos. One got lost and another was shelled and later overrun with at least one man killed and several captured. These men were later recovered from a ship in the Bizerte harbor.

With more from **K** Company of the 47th, Sergeant Burleigh Brewer recalls:

My first impression of the Sedjenane valley was 'What a hell of a place to be.' To the left and left front we saw nothing but tall mountains covered with brush that we had to take from the enemy in order to get to Bizerte. To the right and right front was 'Old Baldy' and more of those numbered hills which we'd have to take in order to reach Ferryville.

Lieutenant Brugger directed me to take two men and scout the Arab shacks that lay across the creek immediately to our front. We entered their thorn-fenced compound and found it deserted. I took a couple of steps inside the hut and in seconds my legs were absolutely black with fleas. I can tell you that we left that compound as fast as if the Germans were after us.

We held our company positions for a number of days, sending out lookouts and constantly patrolling in the battalion sector. It was cold at night so we would team up in twos to sleep. We'd put one shelter half on the ground and cover it with a blanket. On top we'd have another banket and shelter half. We never removed our clothes, not even our shoes.

Corporal McCleary was teamed up with me this night. Our ears were tuned to hear a pin drop. Then some noise awakened me with a start. I rolled to the right with my Tommy gun. McCleary went to the left with his .45. 'Blam!' McCleary's .45 exploded and he shot himself in the foot. Our medics were always quickly on the spot patching us up and not getting much credit for a job well done.

Each night our company would set up outposts of six to a dozen men usually commanded by a sergeant. Once one of the outposts was surprised and two or three men were bayoneted to death and others were taken prisoner. One man escaped and the next day he took a patrol back to recover the dead. He was awarded the Silver Star for this.

Two nights later it was my turn to set up an ambush. I took eleven men into the dark and set them out in pairs astride this path running over a brush-covered hill. All of us had automatic weapons. In the wee hours of this moonlit night there was a noise in the bushes behind our position. My partner and I jumped like cats to either side of an opening in the brush and this man

emerged through the opening. We had our Tommy guns stuck in
each of his ears. He froze and I recognized him as a sergeant
from L Company. When we all got our hearts back in place he
explained his mission and we passed him through.

After we returned to the company in the morning and had a
few hours rest, I noticed the Arabs coming back out of the valley.
I told the guys to get their gear together, we would be jumping off
soon. Those Arabs always seemed to know when an attack was
coming. K Company started out that evening. Incoming shells
burst all around and small arms fire came from the mountain
top which was our objective. It started to rain hard. Fantasti-
cally, hot chili was served us at about 2300 hours. It was raining
so hard you couldn't empty your mess kit. In the morning we
attacked through our own smoke screen and secured the objec-
tive.

1st Lieutenant Charles Scheffel, A Company, 39th Infantry,
recalls of this time:

I reported to the regimental command post after two weeks
at British Battle School. Captain Corpening, the S1, sent me up
to the 1st Battalion which I found by following the commo wire
from regimental headquarters. It was about this time that I
noticed the preponderance of the heavy red German wire leading
everywhere and I realized we'd be up against a highly skilled and
organized defense in this sector.

Gefreiter Karl Schaefer, now living in Netphen, Germany, but
then a member of the lst Kompanie, Tunis 1 Bataillon, remembers:

On Hitler's Birthday, April 20th, our lieutenant called the
platoon back for a pep talk. Since I was the youngest of all I was
left behind on our position to defend it. I had all six machine
guns and a huge amount of hand grenades. This was a dominat-
ing hill position and I could see a large part of of the valley in
front. The road in the valley could not be reached by rifle fire.
Occasionally enemy vehicles rode along it. On this day a column
of vehicles came and stopped. American and English soldiers
dismounted. With binoculars I could see everything quite clearly.
They spread maps and pointed around and gesticulated a lot. I
had the impression that responsibility for a position was to be
turned over from the British to the Americans. However, one of
our neighboring units had also seen what was going on and sent
out a party of about 20 men with one mortar. From my elevation
I could observe everything. The Americans and British were so

occupied with their affairs that they did not notice how they were being encircled. When the ring was closed the mortar coughed four times. These characters, presumably high officers among them, had no choice but to get their hands up. They were then marched back very fast. The vehicles could not be taken along and were blown up with hand grenades.

Captain Alex T. Forrest of the 15th Engineer Battalion recalls:

According to the Royal Engineers the only major problem seemed to be mines. There was also a cratered culvert blown in the road east of Sedjenane between the lines. They had tried to repair it at night only to be driven off by shellfire. Since the British had only been contemplating frontal attacks on Green and Bald Hills, it seemed reasonable that this problem may not have had a high priority. However, I doubted that they had made much of an effort to repair the crater and decided to make a personal reconnaissance of it on Easter Sunday (April 25th). Luck was with me this day. I hit a trip wire stretched across the road between our lines and the crater. Two S-mines jumped up but failed to explode. After my narrow escape from shooting myself at El Guettar and an earlier miracle at Port Lyautey, and now this brush with the mines, I became convinced that I was due to live out the war. The crater was later bridged by our fellows.

They might have put out a sign, "Beware of the Mines." 2nd Lieutenant William O. Rockwood, Battery A, 60th Field Artillery Battalion, remembers:

One day our CO, Doug France, and I set out in a jeep hunting for a neberwerfer battery that had been firing at our position. Suddenly we came under fire of 88s. We found ourselves flat on the ground, luckily not having disturbed anti-personnel mines which were at our fingertips. The firing stopped and there were no casualties. We returned to the jeep to find we had just skirted two land mines in the road. This was the last of our going out looking for trouble.

2nd Lieutenant John J. Wessmiller of Anti-tank Company, 60th Infantry, was another who had a close call early on:

It was a particularly dark night somewhere in the Sedjenane valley and I was not happy with one of my gun positions. Being blessed with excellent night vision I decided to check on it right then and there and Lieutenant Jim Flynn, who had a flashlight with a red lens, followed.

Major General Omar N. Bradley,
Commanding General, II U.S. Corps.
(Army Signal Corps photo.)

> *After wallowing through the thick brush for about ten minutes, I felt my left foot struck by something, hard enough almost to make me lose my balance. I cried out and Jim put his light down and shouted, 'My God, it's a big snake.' I glanced down where the light shown and saw this snake's big rear end sliding off into the brush.*
>
> *I then pulled off my belt and tied it tight around the calf. Jim screamed for a medic and people came running and eventually Major Boyarkin, one of the medics. He flashed a light on my boot and we saw this big glob of slime. He then removed the boot and sock. There on my foot were two dots about a half inch apart, but no blood. The Doc said, 'Wessmiller, you're one of the luckiest guys I know. That was a Black Mamba. I've just been reading about it.'*
>
> *The next morning I prodded the boot around the bite mark and the leather just crumbled away, leaving a big hole.*

On his way to Northern Tunisia General Eddy stopped by the command post of II U.S. Corps and discussed his Division's future employment with General Bradley. The folksy-talking bespectacled Missourian and Eddy hit it off. Bradley was still deputy commander of the Corps but would take over from Patton in a few days. He was friendly, complimentary about the 9th's recent actions and promised that, while it would come under British control temporarily up north, the Divison would be back under his command on April 15th. Regarding the recent fighting at Maknassy and El Guettar, Bradley emphasized that, although Northern Tunisia had more vegetation and cover, seizure and retention of the high ground was still the key to unlocking the German defense. He liked the plan that Eddy had outlined and was unconcerned about the divergence that would develop as the 9th and 1st Divisions progressed in their respective attacks;.

> *'Let me worry about that, Manton,' Bradley stated. 'Go after the enemy on as broad a front as you can manage. The other guy can't be strong everywhere and, when you punch a hole, exploit it as quickly as possible. There's a lot riding on our performance, you know. We have to show everyone that the U.S. Army can whip the Germans on their terms.'*

Eddy was pleased with the meeting. While they had not met previously the two men had spoken on the telephone. By the end of two days of hard fighting at El Guettar, the 9th's commander had lost four of his six battalion commanders without any appreciable effect on the enemy. In a moment of discouragement he telephoned his superior to discuss the problem and the possibility of getting replacements. General Patton was not at his headquarters but the call was taken by his deputy General Bradley who was understanding and sympathetic. Bradley suggested, however, that Eddy ride out the battle with promotions from within the regiments rather than seeking outside help which probably would not arrive in time to be of much help. If this did not solve Eddy's problem, somehow he felt better for having talked it over with the soft-spoken Missourian.[2]

General Eddy was also now aware of Bradley's cool performance when caught at El Guettar by German Stukas. While the planes were still boring in, Bradley was patching up the wounded and getting them evacuated. After his reception at II Corps Headquarters this day Eddy felt like a full-fledged and valued member of the team and not the potential victim of the tempestuous egomaniac that George Patton had shown himself to be.

The 9th's commander also stopped and paid his respects to the British V Corp's commanding general. There were no complaints about the American's relief of their 46th Infantry Division. Eddy thanked all involved for the smooth move of the 9th across the British rear and for the 46th leaving behind officers to show the newcomers their ways about the battleground. The 46th's cooperation could not have been more complete.

Finally, Eddy's driver slowed in front of the 9th's command post sign on the road near the town of Sedjenane. There were two armed Arabs standing in the road saluting and gesturing with the usual arm-sweeps of military policemen directing traffic. The general's eyes stopped popping when he realized that these were his men and then he grinned broadly. "Someone's using their heads to do more than prop up their helmets," he said to no one in particular. The chief of staff met him at the door of the large whitewashed and tiled house that was to be the 9th's new command post.

'We've got a personnel problem,' reported Colonel George B. Barth. He explained that a Lt. Colonel Theodore J. Conway, former aide-de-camp to the army group commander, had been assigned directly to the Division on orders of General Alexander. Conway wanted to fill one of the battalion command jobs presumably vacant by virtue of Maknassy and El Guettar losses.

'Hell's bells, Chief,' Eddy exploded. 'The regimental commanders have already made their selections to fill those slots. I'm not going to order them to make room for this guy.'

'Well, General, he's highly recommended by Lucian Truscott down at 3rd Division. Conway was on the staff there and, before that, with Truscott when he commanded the landing at Port Lyautey.'

Eddy snorted, 'Then why doesn't Truscott give him a job?'

'Because they haven't had any casualties,' Barth said quietly and paused to light his pipe.

General Eddy fumed while his chief of staff fussed and puffed; then the general brightened:

'I'll tell you what we're going to do, Chief. Call Brown, deRohan and Randle and tell them what we've got here. In the next few days I want them to come back one at a time to lunch or dinner. Conway will be seated next to them and they're to have a good look-see. If this hot shot is any kind of a charmer, he'll get himself a job. If nobody wants him, we'll have to figure out something else. They don't have to take him. Make sure Conway understands.[3] *Now, how is the G3 coming along with the field order?'*

'He's ready to brief you, General.'

'Let's do it after dinner.'

The 9th Division's Field Order No. 20, April 20, 1943,[4] ordered the 47th Infantry astride the Sedjenane-Jefna road to demonstrate beginning at 0530 hours on April 23rd in the direction of Djebels el Azzag (Green Hill) and el Ajred (Bald Hill) which the Germans had fortified strongly. By vigorous patrolling and bombardment the 47th would seek to convince the enemy that, notwithstanding other tactical moves of the Division that might be detected, the principal effort would be another assault of their Azzag-Ajred positions.

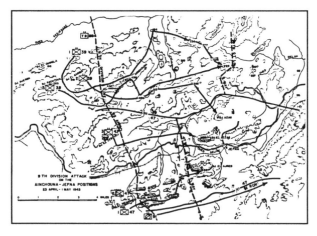

Map 3. 9th Division attack on Ainchouna-Jefna positions.
(From To Bizerte with the II Corps.)

9th Division "Braintrust."
Left to right: Brig. Gen. S. Leroy Irwin, CG Div. Arty.;
Maj. Gen. Manton S. Eddy, Div. CG; Brig. Gen. Donald A. Stroh,
Asst. Div. CG; Col. George B. Barth, C/S.(Army Signal Corps photo.)

Meanwhile, to the north, the 39th Infantry would assault Djebel Ainchouna, a long twin-peaked eminence that would be the key to getting on successive high points culminating with a hill which dominated Jefna and the road to the east from there.

Even further north, after a series of secret night marches from the rear, the 60th Infantry would attack east along the high ground forming the south shoulder of the Sedjenane valley. Its final objective was high ground overlooking the Mateur-Bizerte highway. The attached Corp Franc d'Afrique would advance along the hills separating the Sedjenane valley from the sea, and also end up on high ground covering the highway running from Mateur to Bizerte.

In 1969, Major General (Ret.) George B. Barth, who had been the 9th's chief of staff in Northern Tunisia, wrote about the Division's plan:[5]

> *The plan of attack was determined by the terrain over which we must advance. Every hill must be captured before going on to the next one. We must command the high ground and take enemy observation off our movements and thus destroy the effectivness of his anti-tank defense before committing our armored forces.*
>
> *This we had learned the hard way at El Guettar! We had one great advantage over the previous battle. Except for the strong, prepared positions on Green and Bald Hills which we did not intend to attack frontally, the Germans did not have any dug-in prepared positions until we reached the line of hills that defended the plain of Bizerte and Tunis. It would be an infantry fight at close quarters in rugged 'djebel country.' Except for a paved road from Djefna Station to Mateur, roads were poor or non-existent.*
>
> *A color-layered contour map prepared by the staff brought out the nature of the terrain admirably and determined our tactical plans. It was clear that the dominant hill mass, extending slightly northeast for about fifteen miles and pointing straight towards Bizerte, was Djebel Ainchouna and Kef Nsour. Each high peak along this hill mass must be assaulted and held before the one to the east could be taken. This difficult task was given to the 39th Infantry.*
>
> *The north flank was held by the Corps Franc d'Afrique, a French force of five battalions, including one Tabour (battalion) of Goums.*
>
> *The sector south of this was the responsibility of the 60th Infantry. We were glad to have it back and its strength was vital to us now. The 60th had fought at Maknassy, attached to the 1st Armored Division. The 60th's experience was much the same as*

ours. It had not been strong enough to break through at Maknassy but, while exhausted, it was still intact as a regiment and had gained much battle experience. In the advance on Bizerte it was to become our most outstanding regiment. It took every objective given it and helped the Corps Franc d'Afrique to take theirs. This French force was poorly equipped, as were other French units in Tunisia; (it) had no artillery of its own and few modern machine guns. Without the help of the 60th it could not have succeeded in its advance that finally resulted in the capture of Bizerte. While the hills on our northern front were not as high as those of the Ainchouna or Kef Nsour hill masses, they were covered by dense thickets of briars where hand-to-hand fighting at close range would often be required.

Our right regiment, the 47th Infantry, had the mission of advancing to the base of Green and Bald Hills. (The previous winter in the race for Tunis, the British had splintered a complete brigade on those two hills and had been driven back with heavy casualties. We didn't intend to make the same mistake.)

Between the 47th and our boundary with the 1st Infantry Division was the attached 91st Reconnaissance Squadron, a very mobile force with many automatic weapons. Our line was thinly held here, which was a matter of continuing concern to General Eddy, but we couldn't be strong everywhere and took a calculated risk on our right where the enemy could have broken through but never did. General Eddy did take his division reserve, one battalion of the 47th Infantry, and place it behind the right of the 47th, where it could be used in an emergency to back up the 91st Reconnaissance Squadron.

Field Order No. 20 assigned specific intermediate as well as final objectives to each assaulting unit along with a schedule for their seizure. Resulting from intensive terrain study, the schedule's purpose was to insure that the respective assault units were as mutually supporting as they could be given the wide sectors assigned and the rough terrain to be covered. Thereby, it was considered less likely that one unit would get ahead of the general advance and risk a flank attack and piecemeal defeat by the enemy.

The order also allocated supporting artillery fires, reconnaissance and security tasks to the 9th Reconnaissance Troop, and the attached 91st Reconnaissance Squadron and 894th Tank Destroyer Battalion, as well as support missions for the Division's 15th Engineer Battalion.

The engineering tasks contemplated in the document were so formidable that the 15th's operations officer thought that an engineer regiment would be kept busy. Jeep trails would have to be constructed behind the advancing 39th and 60th Regiments and the CFA as they advanced. There were nothing but foot paths and cart trails existing where these units would go. In addition, the Germans had had plenty of time to indulge their passion for mining approaches to key positions.[6] Finally, the main supply roads to the rear and those projected to become MSRs were never intended to carry the traffic to which they would be subjected as the attack progressed. They would need much maintenance.

Captain Forrest recalls:

> *Sedjenane was a critical crossroads town. Roads ran east to Bizerte and Mateur and north to Cap Serrat. But it was in a bowl, open to observation and interdiction by Jerry. We had to construct a new main supply road taking traffic in defilade around the high intersection. We also built jeep trails from the Sedjenane-Cap Serrat road extending east on either side of the Sedjenane river. Each of our companies' mechanical equipment, a D7 bulldozer and a compressor, was fully employed. In the final analysis, however, it was the gut-busting efforts of the individual engineer to clear brush, pack the roadbed, ensure shoulder stability, etc., that got the job done. Altogether, we built 128 miles of new road in this area and I daresay some are in use today.*

Private Lester Schwear, I Company, 47th Infantry, recalls his first night in the Sedjenane Valley:

> *There we were set up in a cactus patch. D. J. Carter and I had stolen a can of peanut butter from the cooks and went to sleep with full bellies. About midnight we heard something and lit a cigarette lighter. Guess what! The biggest rats we'd ever seen were at our heads. That can flew out of our pup tent.*
>
> *The next day here comes two fighter planes, a German with a British Spitfire on his tail. The boys all cut loose and down came the Spitfire. Orders came down. No more firing at planes.*

Pfc. Kenneth L. Meyer, 9th Military Police Company, recalls:

> *The main route from Algiers to Bizerte came through Beja where an alternate route branched north to Sedjenane and then to the east. A detail, of which I was a part, directed traffic at the intersection. About a half-mile north of this point there was a bridge over a deep chasm. German Stukas were trying to knock out this bridge in order to interrupt the 9th's supply.*
>
> *The bridge was protected by several quad .50s. When they*

were all firing they put out a lot of rounds and made a grand racket.

Our little campground was about 150 yards from the intersection where the traffic turned to head for Sedjenane. We usually slept in a building's basement but that was very humid. On one particularly warm night a few of us had decided to sleep outside. About 2 A.M. a terrible roar woke us and we ran for the building since the debris coming down from those quad .50s could be bad for a guy's health. A few minutes later we sheepishly realized that our anti-aircraft barrage was only a 6x6 downshifting to approach the bridge.

The river under the bridge was too cold for bathing but we discovered there were hot springs in the vicinity. One with a pool about the size of a bathtub was located about 100 yards from our bridge. I was bathing there one day, singing away as I lathered up. Suddenly all the quad .50s opened up. Tracers began flying back and forth, I looked up to see a Stuka at about 6,000 feet just starting its dive at the bridge.

'Meyer,' I said, 'this ain't no place for you,' and I headed downstream, stark naked, hair blowing in the breeze, running and stumbling as fast as feet would take me.

To this day I claim that the Stuka pilot saw me and laughed so hard that his aim was off. This is how the bridge at Beja was saved.

The Luftwaffe was still very much in evidence during the early days in the Sedjenane area. Captain Herbert W. Clegg, S1 of the 2nd Battalion, 47th Infantry, recollects:

A few hours after the battalion arrived in the Sedjenane valley and had, we thought, pretty well camouflaged our trucks in a wadi, the Luftwaffe found us and bombed our position. We all dove under the trucks and no one was hurt badly. However, I received my only wounds of the war, a small piece of shrapnel in the back and another in my hand.

Pfc. Duane Olson, operations clerk of Headquarters, 47th Infantry, recalls:

We established the 47th's CP in the dead of night on the slopes just in rear of the forward battalions.

Our mess sergeant was named MacAlister. He was a rawboned Kentuckian with a visage that would frighten a priest and his human relation techniques were severely rationed. I doubt if Mac could read menus too well but he had a natural flair with the saltshaker and herbs so the food was edible. Above all, Mac detested one of his kitchen crew, a soldier named Walker.

Walker was an anomaly; intelligence quotient of 134, college graduate, test scores in the high 140s, slouchy, unkempt. He detested his intellectual inferior, Sergeant MacAlister. Of course it was no contest for Walker would bait Mac. Mac would get trapped. Walker would taunt and Mac would burn and throw every dirty job Walker's way. Mac's cursing took on some creative characteristics that yielded a clue to some inate intelligence never manifested in his ordinary behavior.

The night of our move the kitchen truck crept up the hill in total darkness. Surprisingly, noise of its movement was minimal. My buddy and I had come earlier on the CP truck and located our pup tent between some rocks that would serve as barriers to those coming later. Still, the kitchen truck came very close and the whispered commands of MacAlister could be heard, mostly directed at Walker with the usual salutation, 'Walker, you eff-up,' or 'Walker, you mothereffer, keep quiet. Watch your effing mouth,' all as the truck carefully ground its gears to a final stop.

Then came the cataclysm. Down with the tailgate. Admonitions to unload with care. 'Watch those big pots.' Then, all of a sudden a pot came loose, followed by another, and another, clanging reverberating across the entire hillside. A final clang and deathly silence for at least a minute. Then, in a stage whisper worthy of Old Vic, came the horrible indictment: 'Walker, you effing prick!' And so it went.

Also in the Jefna area about this time, Assistant G2, Captain Dean T. Vanderhoef remembers:

I was riding my motorcycle headed back one day from the CP after visiting a recon outfit to our south. Daydreaming, I came around a curve and in front of me was a jeep wrecked from hitting a mine. I came screeching to a halt and it dawned on me that I was in plain view of the Jerrys on Bald and Green Hills looming just ahead. I'll never forget the panic with which I turned that two-ton Harley around in that well mined road. My horse cavalry-learned vocabulary got a good work out when I found the dug in soldier who had let me go by. Said he: 'I didn't want to give my position away.'

Pfc. Raymond M. Connolly, 9th Signal Company, remembers:

I distinctly remember the God-awsome artillery barrages

laid down in an area north and west of the railroad bridge in Sedjenane. We were holed up near there and it seemed we would never move out. The area had been heavily fought over in the past. At one point my buddy and I came across the half-buried bodies of British infantrymen. The sight has never left me. It's always reminded me of the brutality of armed conflict and the cheapness of life.

Sergeant Barney Angell, B Company, 15th Engineer Battalion, remembers:

Late in April we were in the Bald Hill area. This high ground commanded the road leading to Jefna and Bizerte and the enemy, from an OP on it, was ready to bring down fire on any movement. It was here I met the Catholic Father Edward T. Connors.

I was assigned to reconnoiter daily a bridge on the road near old Baldy. It was mined with big Tellers. The Germans would not fire on one or two men snooping about as long as we did not touch the mines. One day a jeep carrying three U.S. sailors looking for souvenirs came sailing past the road guard. They were all killed in the explosion at the bridge. Our medics went charging up to help and drew heavy fire from the mountain.

The sailors' bodies had lain out there several days when Father Connors came to B Company and asked the C.O. if someone could help him get the bodies out with a litter party. He agreed it would have to be done at night. I got the job. It did not make me feel any better to be forbidden to carry arms because of the red crosses.

On the night selected we started out together but soon lost the litter bearers. The good Father and I were all alone. We picked up each body and carried it back about 300 yards to where we found the medics ready to take over.

Until he died I had a letter every year from Father Connors reminding me of our adventure together and telling me of his annual memorial mass in Worcester. This fine brave man took a lot of kidding from the guys about my being his protestant prospect.

1st Lieutenant Jack A. Dunlap, B Company, 39th Infantry, recalls:

Upon arrival in the Sedjenane area our company relieved a British parachute unit. One of their officers was left behind to familiarize us with the terrain and to show us their routine patrol routes. I became the company patrol officer and formed four and five-man patrol groups. We patrolled each day out one to three miles in front of our positions. The British officer pointed out several clusters of Arab huts, some of which he considered friendly and others unfriendly. I carried extra cigarettes for the friendlies as a means of getting information on enemy sightings but, despite their endorsement, I never really trusted them fully.

A few days before the final drive through the mountains I was given a patrol mission to bring in some prisoners. I beefed up my patrol to nine men and set out shortly after daylight. At the last moment I was asked to take along a new officer so that he could gain the experience. We penetrated almost twice as far on this mission as we had gone previously. Finally, a two-man German outpost was spotted on a knoll across a little valley. We were able to work our way across the valley and behind them. We had complete surprise and quickly bundled the two back the way we had come to the first shelter. There to my dismay I discovered that two of my men, Ervin and Campbell, had gone back to retrieve the weapons taken from the prisoners. The new officer had directed this.

All we could do was to wait for their return but after about ten minutes, from that direction came the unmistakable chatter of German burp guns. I then turned to Corporal Harris, my most experienced man, and told him to return the prisoners to our positions by the most direct route. I relieved Harris of all but two clips of M1 ammo and cautioned him that, if the prisoners gave him any trouble, he was to shoot one immediately; the other wouldn't give him any trouble after that. I made sure the Germans understood.

The patrol then maneuvered back to the knoll where we had captured the men. Almost there we came across Campbell's body. He had been shot through the head. We searched the area for Erwin but couldn't find him. In the meantime a German formation was spotted. I moved the patrol into a defiladed position but quickly realized we were no match for the enemy. Since we hadn't been detected, we were able to back away and take a circuitous route back to B Company's positions, arriving the next morning. Corporal Harris had already returned with the two prisoners. Erwin appeared later that day. The reason we had not found him was that he had found a drainage ditch and crawled back to the German's rear. Then he stole some Arab's cloak and walked nonchalantly back to the company area. Campbell was the first man killed in an outfit for which I was responsible. It left an indelible impression.

1st Lieutenant Lewis E. Maness, commanding G Company, 47th Infantry, recollects:

> *It took us several days to reach our destination in the Sedje-nane sector where we relieved a company of the York and Lancashire Regiment of the 138th Brigade. The relief was made at night. I was met by a British captain who looked twice my age and the guide I had sent forward with the Battalion's advance party. The Britisher told me that since he had learned the Yank company was considerably larger than his, he had sufficient extra holes dug so that every one of my men would have one. I have often wondered, if the situation had been reversed, I would have been as courteous. The British captain also left us his executive officer, a Leftenant Olson, who remained for a few days showing us around and accompanying our patrols. This was a tremendous help, particularly in orienting us on the wire and minefields of both sides. When Olson left, we loaded him down with C-rations and American cigarettes.*
>
> *We stayed in these positions for a while, sending out patrols each night but we never found the German front line. Once our patrol met a German patrol. A fire fight developed without casualties to our side. The Germans shelled our positions from time to time and our artillery fired back.*
>
> *One day before the offensive started the British insisted that we 'green Americans' must witness a demonstration of their fire and movement technique for taking an enemy position, what they called 'battle drill.' Our company provided the demonstration troops and British officers made the presentation to the assembled officers of our Battalion. It was not unlike the standard Fort Benning show of laying down a base of fire while maneuvering an assault unit around one flank. Our men were happily firing away with live ammo and this, apparently, woke up the Krauts who began throwing artillery into our midst. Needless to say, this broke up the class and we scattered for our holes.*
>
> *We were in our inherited positions for about ten days and then moved east and dug in before Bald and Green Hills. Here we resumed patrolling and exchanged mortar and artillery fire with the enemy but our casualties remained at zero.*

Pfc. Charles E. Hoffman, B Company, 15th Engineer Battalion, remembers waiting for the attack:

We were camped by a British engineer supply point just off the main road. One day a bunch of quartermaster trucks pulled into our area and parked bumper-to-bumper. When warned about Jerry planes that were still coming around, the drivers said they'd only be a minute. Not long after that we heard the roar of a diving plane and the sound of German machine guns. We dove for a dry stream bed and hugged one bank and then the other as two Jerries strafed and bombed back and forth. When it was over the cry, 'Medic!' sounded and we found Lieutenant Ware, our platoon leader, had been hit. He was badly wounded and that night we learned he had died at the hospital, the first officer from our battalion killed in the war.

Captain Robert J. Sating, 84th Field Artillery Battalion surgeon, wrote nearly every day to his wife back in Cleveland, Ohio:

April 22: The towns I've seen lately haven't told me much, but at one time the life here must have been very rural, peaceful and about 100 years behind us. Now these slumbering villages are nothing but burnt and blasted ruins, a doorway here, a slant-ing roof partially burnt, streets of rough paving block pock-marked with huge holes. A scene of utter devastation . . . Know-ing you're safe from these terrible things is a wonderful feeling.

April 24: I'm so very tired of lying in a damp, dark foxhole in the dead of night and hearing the planes overhead and wonder-ing whether the next egg he drops will be curtains for you, or whether you'll see the dawn of a new day and begin ducking all over again . . . I imagine people are ducking all over the world and not just me. The only thing is it seems that bomb is meant just for you.

2nd Lieutenant Orion C. Shockley, Cannon Company, 47th Infantry, recalls:

After arriving in the area I located an observation post in our sector and began firing. I had been firing from there for two days when Colonel Brown and his staff from the 39th Infantry came up. The colonel insisted that I was not where I said I was on the map and threated to court-martial me for trying to mis-lead him. He had led his regiment into a position over two miles from where they were supposed to be and refused to admit that he could be wrong. I finally got a message through to Colonel Randle who asked my location. When I told him he said, 'Wait right there and I will come to where you have told me.' A short time later Randle came roaring up. Brown's face fell but he still

*argued with Randle. I believe General Eddy got into the fracas
but it turned out that I was right. After all, how could I have
directed fire if I had not known my position?*

After the war Brigadier General Edwin H. Randle, the 47th
Infantry's commander in Africa, wrote of his experiences:[7]

*It was late in April, 1943. While waiting for the final attack
the Colonel's command post was in a forester's cottage on the
road to Jefna Station, only a few miles west of Bizerte. He had
taken over the cottage from a British brigadier named Harding
whose brigade the 47th had relieved. Knowing the 47th's companies were larger than his, Brigadier Harding had extra holes dug,
and he left behind two British NCO's with each company to
familarize the men with the terrain and where the enemy was.*

*The forester's cottage was near the main road so the Colonel
had visitors. Two sightseeing medical officers in a jeep did not
stop for information and got themselves blown up by a German
mine for their pains.*

*Other visitors had more sense and experience. They included
Generals Clark and Huebner. But the one, it turned out, he was
happiest to see was his own division commander. Early one
afternoon, just before the final attack, General Eddy came and
without beating around the bush, said, 'Randle, I've recommended you for the DSC and to be promoted to brigadier general.' Both barrels, just like that. The colonel was overcome.
Either one would have been just great. The Distinguished Service
Cross ranked next to the Medal of Honor and relatively few were
awarded. But it and promotion to general too; that left him
speechless. Afterwards he felt sure General Eddy must have
thought him an ungrateful clod to not even say thank you, but for
the moment he was stunned.*

Notes

1. George F. Howe, *Northwest Africa: Seizing the Initiative in the
West*, p. 616.

2. General Eddy's telephone calls from his headquarters were
monitored and logged by officers of the 9th Signal Company. Lt. Col.
Herbert Lott, USA (Ret.), recalled this one.

3. General Theodore J. Conway retired from the Army in 1968 after a distinguished career culminating with U.S. Strike Command. As usual for a retiring officer of his rank, he was invited to the Army's Military History Institute, Carlisle, PA, to participate in its oral history program. A transcript of his interview is on file in MHI's library and it recounts the incident reported here. Conway, incidentally, did not get the battalion command job he was seeking. Each regimental commander turned him down. He then returned to General Alexander's headquarters but, as we shall see, an assignment to the 9th was eventually his.

4. *Report of Operation Conducted by 9th Inf. Div., USA, Northern Tunisia, 11 April-8 May 1943* (National Archives, Washington, DC).

5. George B. Barth, *The Octofoil Division Comes of Age in World War II,* p. 17. (Unpublished manuscript in files of the author.)

6. Howe, *op. cit.* p. 614: "Defiles between hills and approaches up the slopes and in the draws were freely sown with anti-personnel mines. Routes likely to be used by American patrols and good observation points which the enemy would have to evacuate as he retired, were also heavily mined. The 47th Infantry, for example, found one small area 500 by 100 feet in which as many as 600 mines had been placed."

7. Edwin H. Randle, *Safi Adventure,* p. 216. Colonel Randle had an aversion to using the first person in his writing.

RAIDERS RUMBLE

Colonel Randle's delicate mission with his 47th Infantry in the Jefna corridor was to demonstrate but not to be drawn into battle against the Germans' prepared defenses on Green and Bald Hills. Between April 13, when the regiment relieved the British 138th Brigade, until D-Day, April 23rd, its 3rd Battalion (Captain Gordon H. Sympson) and 1st Battalion (Major Wendell T. Chaffin), patrolled vigorously the hilly terrain of "No Man's Land." They were trying to pursuade the enemy that the Americans had the capability as well and the intent of breaking through at any time. The 47th's pressure was also intended to allay any suspicion that the 9th Division's main effort was flanking to the north with the 39th and 60th Regiments.

Staff Sergeant Robert S. McCully of L Company remembers of this activity:

> *After we relieved the English the company commander sent my platoon on a combat patrol toward Green Hill. We ran into a buzz saw. Enemy machine guns were firing all around us. When word came to get out only eight of us made it. Over half the men were captured.*

1st Lieutenant Robert E. Hulslander, executive officer of I Company, had a more successful experience:

> *A few days after we took over the British positions we split our force. Captain Tanner took part of the unit to outpost a hill*

north of our position and I was left in charge of the base. Shortly after they reported they were established came one of those messages like Custer sent Captain Reno, 'The Germans are coming. Come quick!'

Although our route went right through a minefield we could see the path left by Tanner's force so this obstacle did not slow us any. We got there just before the Germans did and, with the help of friendly artillery and our battalion's 81s, their attack was broken up. We went after the enemy when they withdrew but they had disappeared.

Colonel Randle was quite upset about this loss of contact. We were ordered to send out an officer-led patrol, 'to go as far as necessary to find the enemy!' I got the job and decided to head for the top of Green Hill. Surely there would be Germans there.

Five of us moved out and reached the base of Green Hill without incident about 3 P.M. While enroute I spotted and reported some movement on the top of the hill. Captain Tanner ordered me to keep going.

We found a continuous band of single-apron barbed wire fence at the base of Green Hill which we cut and passed through where it went across an Arab cemetery. I was very uneasy as it was now obvious we could be seen from the hilltop where I had noticed movement. My radioman was calling the captain to report our passage of the fence when I saw a German soldier rise from the grass only 40 yards away. He had heard the radio but hadn't spotted us yet. We began to fire wildly, ducking between the grave markers when the Germans returned our fire. They began popping up all over the place and we got out of there in a hurry.

We all got back safely about dark. Captain Tanner said the colonel was very pleased that contact with the enemy had been restored.

1st Lieutenant Robert H. Pettee, S3 of the 3rd Battalion, recalls learning the difference between "cover" and "concealment" at about this time:

The two words are used together so frequently that one might think they were interchangable. Not so. On the forward slope of a small hill we occupied west of Jefna there was a fair sized clump of bushes where I found myself with one of the artillery observers. The lieutenant was registering and it was pretty quiet. After a while we had more company. Someone suggested coffee and it was getting downright sociable when we were rudely inter-

rupted by the enemy's 47mm shellfire. We left our 'concealment' in a hurry and headed behind the hill for 'cover.' I recall finding Lieutenant Jim Neeley there laughing fit to die at the spectacle we had provided. He offered a drink from his canteen which, happily, contained something more restorative than plain water.

1st Lieutenant J. Edel Clark of the Regiment's Antitank Company recalls:

On the afternoon of April 23rd things were quiet and I was writing a V-mail home when a message came through on the radio that Captain Adams and Lieutenants Hayes and O'Keefe were seriously wounded and being evacuated. They had been out reconnoitering for new positions.

I jumped in the jeep and found them at the collecting station. Adams and Hayes were clearly headed for the States. O'Keefe was not so bad and eventually came back to us. They had gotten into a field of 'Bouncing Betty' S-mines and set one off. It was enough to lay them all low.

German defenses in the area were manned by three battalions of the 160th Panzer Grenadier Regiment which, notwithstanding its heavyweight name, was in effect a cadre organization barely able to control its three unusual infantry units. These were so-called "Tunis Feld" or "Afrika" replacement battalions which were originally intended to be located behind the lines feeding replacements as required to the line divisions. As losses became heavier for the Germans in Tunisia, the battalions themselves, at full strength with about 900 men, were fed directly into the line and even organized as regiments as in this instance. While the 160th had had the experience of participating in the Division Manteuffel's February offensive, its heavy losses then had not been fully replaced. Its components were the 1st and 4th Tunis Battalions on Green Hill and the 30th Africa Battalion on Bald Hill.

Also in the Jefna neighborhood was the 11th Parachute Engineer Battalion (Major Rudolf Witzig,) the Manteuffel's Division's reserve at this time.

Sergeant Gordon E. Herwig, A Company, will never forget his platoon's run-in with some of those German paratroopers:

The morning after the British left us Lieutenant Paul R. Buffalo's 1st Platoon outposted a knob immediately west of Bald Hill. We stopped at the supply vehicle on our way out to pick up extra grenades, three bandoliers of rifle ammo and three days of C-rations. Each man was carrying two canteens of water.

It was a long walk with my squad leading. All was quiet until we approached our objective. Then the Krauts began to mortar and shell the near slope and the ravines on either side. Lieutenant Buffalo came up and directed our approach. It was a fast move but the platoon stayed spread out and didn't panic. As soon as we started up the objective's back side the German shelling stopped.

Digging in on the knob was frustrating because the soil was so thin. We could only get down a couple of inches and then had to pile up rocks to get any protection. My squad was on the right.

The first night was quiet. On the next day we made some moves which drew a mortar response. During the second night another squad patrolled up Bald Hill until they drew fire. They had no casualties. Before dawn I checked my outpost and Browning automatic rifle (BAR) position. The sun was coming up. I was just opening a can of rations when all hell broke loose.

A German light machine gun split the air with a sound like a tearing bed sheet. Thank the Lord I had a good BAR crew. They immediately began firing down the slope at the Germans advancing from our rear. I threw a grenade. Others followed.

It was all over quickly. While the BAR crew kept us covered my assistant squad leader and I found seven dead and dying Germans. I was nauseated and the corporal was white as a sheet. Then Lieutenant Buffalo arrived and raised hell with us for letting the Germans get so close. He assumed they came around our flank. We were ordered to bury the dead, first searching the bodies for anything of intelligence value. Also, he laid it on us that our squad would patrol to Bald Hill that night.

Later in the afternoon my platoon leader returned and apologized for his remarks. He had tracked the Germans back and learned that they had come across our wire far to the rear and followed it into the position. He realized we couldn't have spotted them any earlier than we did and said we'd done a first-rate job.

We made our patrol that night without incident, finding everything on Bald Hill as our earlier patrols had reported. There were three pill boxes and we fired on each without response. We then put up a flare. Again, nothing.

1st Lieutenant Lawrence J. McLaughlin, A Company's executive officer, recalls:

Early on the outposts of the 47th had not fared well with the German patrols. A couple were captured and Colonel Randle, our CO, was quite upset about it. He received the news of our 1st Platoon's success with great pleasure and his congratulations to Lieutenant Buffalo were profuse.

After the action with the German patrol we instituted a strict challenge and password regimen. One night our ration party was stopped at the perimeter with the challenge 'Tiger.' The password was 'Lion' but the leader of the group, who had a tendency to stutter, could not get it out. After increasingly desperate moments, he blurted out 'Rag!' A few laughs and they were admitted. After all, we were hungry.

Staff Sergeant Howard D. Brooks, C Company, mostly remembers the beauty of the view from their first positions:

We were spread out on the south shoulder of the valley. The foreground was covered with sword grass spangled with red poppies and bright blue cup-shaped flowers about an inch wide with a conspicuous white throat. The groundcover was about a foot high. In the valley's center were several large low sprawling tents of nomads which were woven from the goathair or sheep's wool of their herds. There were a number of half-wild dogs roving about. Around their tents the natives had stacked thorn bushes as fence.

As soon as we were settled, the CO, Lieutenant Burton Anderson, asked me to accompany him on reconnaissance. We followed a track leading east from the position, stopping frequently and making sure to stay off the skyline. When we neared the Arab tents the dogs raised a racket.

The wind rose as it got dark and the sword grass was being tossed about making a continuous sighing-swishing sound so that we couldn't hear much else. After a while we packed it in. Later the night became balmy with the sky full of stars but no moon.

Our company had a five-man outpost with a BAR out to the left front that night. At some point a German patrol came in and captured them. That news shook up the platoon. Anderson and I realized that while we were working our way out on the right, the Germans may well have been coming in on the left of our sector.

Sergeant Frank Brusic, a mortar observer of D Company, saw some action:

I remember one morning spotting a whole platoon of Germans just settling down to eat. I zeroed with a round well off to their right and then shifted to fire for effect. I know we hurt them for shortly we were subjected to a terrific artillery barrage.

One day I was asked to fire on a suspected enemy position just forward of C Company. There was no observation possible because the growth was so thick in this place. I brought the rounds in by sound alone and then fired for effect. When I came down from the OP that night they told me that some C Company guys had been by with blood in their eyes for my almost killing them. It was a long time before we were again asked for such close-in support.

The 47th's D-Day was signalled by a further advance by the lst Battalion to the ridge based on Hill 605 which bore the road running south from the highway at A'ouna Station. These moves continued until on May 3rd Major Chaffin's troops were on Hills 501 and 533 poised to assault Bald Hill now only a few hundred yards away.

Corporal Eduard Bleck of A Company had a remarkable experience while this was going on:

There were five of us in a wadi approaching the south side of Bald Hill when suddenly we were looking up the rifle barrels of a bunch of Germans. They were the crew of an 88mm gun well dug-in and camouflaged but without wheels. They were very polite in relieving us of our weapons and especially our rations. They really enjoyed that food. We stayed the night. About noon the next day they turned us loose and, after a long hike, we caught up with the rest of our company.

On the top of Bald Hill that day a medic named Miller and I were watching trucks and troops detouring around a crater in the main highway which ran by down below. There was an explosion when one of the soldiers stepped on a mine. We slid down to give aid. The guy was screaming. His leg was nearly gone. Miller told me to hold him and, as I watched, he cut the leg off at the knee with his pocket knife.

Meanwhile north of the highway, the 3rd Battalion was seeking to flank Green Hill from the north. Moving more slowly than the lst in its somewhat less rugged but even more densely vegetated sector, it occurred to Colonel Randle that Captain Sympson had not had sufficient time in command to develop the kind of staff that could sustain the unit's more rapid advance. He therefore had his adjutant, Captain Herman A. Schmidt, become the 3rd Battalion's executive officer.

2nd Lieutenant William H. Horan, K Company, recalls of his battalion's activity:

On April 28th the 3rd Battalion moved about two miles east and took up another position. No opposition was encountered. Again we patrolled or moved small units about to organize various positions so as to keep the enemy's attention. For example, my platoon was sent two miles forward to occupy a small knob. A section of M Company's machine guns and the 60mm mortar section of our own Weapons Platoon were attached. Our movement got the Jerry's attention. We were heavily shelled when we reached our objective but this tapered off as we dug in.

Looking back across the valley to the main K Company positions one could appreciate the advantages enjoyed by the German observers. Runners were seen coming and going from what had to be a command post. Suddenly this area blossomed and was torn apart by exploding shells; a heavy price to pay for poor camouflage discipline.

Soon after this we were ordered to return and take up new positions on the left flank. Now I noticed the troops taking great care in digging those positions and disposing of the fresh soil so that enemy observers might pass us by.

Our general mission continued to be patrolling toward Green Hill. On three different occasions company-size patrols went out at night toward that enemy stronghold in an attempt to draw fire and uncover targets. They would get as close as possible to the German positions and then on signal plaster them with everything at hand, including artillery. Usually only ineffective light fire was returned. For one thing, the German machine guns were not sited for close-in work so their return fire would sail back over our heads. When the party was over, back we'd go to our holes, arriving at dawn, hungry and tired.

The terrain and vegetation were terrific challenges to our ingenuity, perseverance and fortitude. The thorny, interlaced brush was nearly inpenetrable. Because of the enemy's commanding positions most of our moves were at night. Everything-- supplies, weapons, ammunition, rations and casualties had to be hand-carried. Cold C-rations were the norm.

A prisoner captured near Green Hill reported that after having been wounded in Russia he was sent to Africa for a rest. He had brand new equipment, including a Mauser rifle with a beautiful stock and a perfect blue job. I coveted the piece but someone else got it first.

On April 30 the 3rd Battalion reached an assault position on the north slope of Green Hill and that night a patrol got to the top unopposed.

1st Lieutenant James E. Leopold of E Company led one of the patrols sent forward by the 2nd Battalion (Captain James D. Johnston) at about this time:

> On the night of May 2nd I was told to take a patrol east along the railroad tracks leading to Jefna. The patrol consisted of four volunteers and we left at 2000 hours. By dawn we had reached a point between Green and Bald Hills without making contact and I decided to climb Bald Hill to the south. When nearing the top we came across trip-wires and mines. By now it was light enough to see the buildings of Jefna a couple of miles further east. There were some indications that the Germans had left, mostly because it was so quiet.
>
> We returned and I reported to Colonel Randle at his CP. He directed me to go to the 1st Battalion and guide them up to Bald Hill. We were in the process of this when orders came to assemble. We were moving out by truck to take part in the final assault on Bizerte.

2nd Lieutenant Frank R. Veno, Headquarters Company, 1st Battalion, remembers:

> While we were poised to assault Bald Hill our OP spotted a German soldier in position there who dutifully every morning got out of his hole and went down the hillside to relieve himself. Somehow this indelicacy brought out the killer instinct of one of our officers but the fact that this German was out of rifle range did not deter him. He borrowed a mule and spent an entire night going back to the truck park and bringing forward one of the .50 caliber machine guns with its ground mount. He got it into position in time and, when the German dropped his drawers, 'Killer' pressed the trigger. The gun malfunctioned. By the time it was fixed the target was gone and later that day we were ordered to move.

As early as May 1st, Colonel Randle planned for a coordinated move of his 1st and 3rd Battalions to seize Green and Bald Hills but this was suspended by orders from II Corps pending its reshuffle of units south of the 9th Division sector. Meanwhile, the division's reconnaissance troop moved south to work with the attached 91st Reconnaissance Squadron in filling a gap which had developed between the 47th Infantry and the adjoining 34th Infantry Division.

This matter of a gap or an open flank was such a concern to General Eddy that he took it up repeatedly with the corps commander. Bradley reacted somewhat sarcastically and in that man's mind, Eddy became pegged forever as a "cautious commander." As Bradley later recorded in his first memoir, *A Soldier's Story*:[1]

> *Before the attack jumped off I went out by jeep to see the division commanders and have a look at their terrain. It was my second visit to Manton Eddy's CP up in the Sedjenane valley where the MP's directing traffic wore Arab burnooses so as not to betray his location to enemy air.*
>
> *A nine-mile gap had been left in the Corps line between Eddy's sector in the north and Terry Allen's advance in the south. Although we patrolled this gap with a reconnaissance force, Eddy confessed that he was uneasy about this wide exposure of his right flank.*
>
> *'Manton,' I reassured him, 'nothing's going to come through that gap. Why Bill Kean [Bradley's chief of staff] and I will go up with rifles to stop anything that might squeeze through.'*
>
> *Eddy smiled but he was unconvinced. When he protested that the enemy could slip a battalion or even a regiment through, I was forced to admit that he could. 'But what could he do even if he did get through,' I said. 'There's nothing there but mountains and scrub thicket; there's not a single road through the gap. Even battalions won't go far if they can't move their trucks behind them.'*
>
> *We could not have plugged that gap without spreading our attacking forces too thinly elsewhere on the Corps front. I took a calculated risk in leaving that gap open. Despite Manton's apprehensions, the enemy never made a move to come through. He was far too busy holding his front together.*

Later in his book Bradley continues:

> *On Easter Sunday (April 25th) I motored up to the Sedjenane for a conference with Eddy. His CP tent had been dug deeply into the ground near a 'Long Tom' artillery position. Each time the battery fired, his tent top shivered as the shells rushed overhead.*
>
> *Despite my frequent assurances Manton still fretted over that open right flank. Thereafter I discovered that he would require an occasional visit from Corps to put his mind at rest. For the moment he would accept my logic on the improbability of an enemy attack, but within a few days the doubts would recur and Eddy would ask for another visit from Corps.*
>
> *The uneasiness, however, did not slow or hamper the astonishing success of Eddy's attack. With a regiment to contain the*

Jefna position, and harry its defenders from the front, Eddy had maneuvered to the left of the Jefna position to gain a strategic position on its north and rear. By May 2 his gains commanded the solitary German exit from that position. The German could either stick to his position and starve or he could abandon it without further resistance. He decided to run out, which he did before Eddy could close the escape road with his infantry.

In the limited sense that the 47th's operation before Jefna did not hold Manteuffel's only reserve in place, then it can be said to have failed. By the same token, the elaborate process by which the 60th Infantry was brought forward to its attack position in order to gain surprise can be chalked up as another tactical failure. The Germans realized the threat and responded to it thereby weakening their Jefna position. Colonel Randle apparently did not detect this; in any event it caused no acceleration of his advance. Probably, that open right flank was doing more than cause Eddy anxiety. As it developed, the failure to hold Witzig in place, or to move the 60th into place undetected, did not make any difference as the German forces were so weak. It is interesting to guess, however, what might have been had Witzig's battalion been stronger.

There was apparently some disappointment on General Bradley's part that Eddy failed to hold the Jefna defenders so that they could have been destroyed rather than permitted to evacuate and fight again another day. However, there is no evidence which would suggest that the replacement battalions of the 160th Panzer Grenadier Regiment ever stood again until their surrender. Most likely the remnants of these formations drifted back to Mateur, to be gobbled up there in the lst Armored Division's attacks.

Notwithstanding what might have been at Jefna, the fact is that a new imperative entered General Bradley's game in late April. From messages coming down from 18th Army Group and First British Army it became clear to the II Corps Commander that earlier assurances that Bizerte was to be the American's exclusive prize might not hold up. Bradley now saw himself in a horse race. Speedy execution became the name of the game![2]

Colonel George B. Barth, the 9th's chief of staff, describes this new imperative:[3]

I remember so well the strong pressure of General Bradley on the 9th Division about May 1st. He called our command post at Sedjenane but General Eddy was up with Conway on the 60th Infantry front so he talked with me personally. He made it crystal clear that we must capture the Djebel Cheniti position as soon as possible and not later than May 5th, using the entire division and all of the artillery on our front, if necessary. He said that, as soon as Cheniti was taken, he wanted a rapid advance made to put the American troops into Bizerte. While he didn't say so in those words, he strongly implied that he wanted American troops to enter Bizerte ahead of the British who were driving for Tunis. He indicated that, while the formal entry into Bizerte was to be made by the Corps Franc d'Afrique and the town turned over to them as soon as they could get there, American troops were not to wait for the French but were to drive for Bizerte with all speed.

The strange adventure of 2nd Lieutenant John P. Ryan of the 9th's G2 Section seems to bear out Bradley's suspicions:

During the Sedjenane operation a French navy captain came through our lines under a flag of truce and I translated for the G2. The captain represented Admiral Derrien who was in charge of the French naval facilities in Bizerte. and known to be pro-Vichy. They wanted an American officer to return with the captain and protect their headquarters from the anticipated fury of the British who they assumed would capture Bizerte. I got the assignment.

As the way to Bizerte was shorter through British lines our passage was arranged. We had a large French flag flying from the front of the car which the British and the Germans respected. I was at the French naval headquarters in Bizerte from May 4 to May 8 while fighting raged outside the city then being heavily bombed. I noted and reported that German paratroopers were in the city and on high ground across the water channel leading from Lake Bizerte to the sea. It was interesting too that the French were quite aware of the Corps Franc d'Afrique which was attached to the 9th.

I was alone with the French until May 6th when that night two British officers worked their way to the headquarters. They stopped the French from drinking their nightly toast to Marshal Petain and his regime in Vichy. The French would not speak to them because the British had attacked French ships at Dakar and Oran earlier in the war. I worked hard to keep the peace and was happy to see our troops arrive in the city on May 8th.

Notes

1. Omar N. Bradley, *A Soldier's Story,*, pp. 80-81.

2. Howe, *Northwest Africa,* p. 653. Howe indicates that Bradley's motivation was strictly to forestall sabotage of Bizerte's port facilities.

3. Barth, *The Octofoil Division Comes of Age,* p. 23.

FALCONS KICK-OFF

Djebel Ainchouna cannot be ignored. It is a formidable piece of terrain extending eastward for about two miles as the south shoulder of the Sedjenane river valley. While not containing the highest point in the area, it is the most massive and heads straight for the critical terrain in the 9th Division's zone of advance. Its two peaks, the western of 432 meters, and the other, 438 meters high and 1,000 meters further along the ridge, were dubbed "Little Ainchouna" and "Big Ainchouna."

Colonel Brown, the 39th's commander, went forward on reconnaissance soon after his units relieved the British lst Parachute Brigade on Djebels el Oumela and Rachtouil. From the British as well as from an attached battalion of the Corps Franc d'Afrique, Brown learned the tactical significance of the Ainchouna massif and the relative weakness of the German forces occupying parts of it. With his S3, Major H. Price Tucker, he closely examined the foreground and discovered the observation and firebase possibilities of Djebels el Hamra (267 meters) and Garcia (291). Since it seemed obvious that Djebel Ainchouna would be assigned as an objective for the regiment in the forthcoming attack, Brown determined that his forces should occupy el Hamra and Garcia in advance of the assault scheduled for April 23rd.

Colonel J. Trimble Brown was the son of a wealthy Philadelphia family and a graduate of Culver Military Academy. He commenced an Army career in 1926. Among his pre-war assignments were two as aide-de-camp to Major General Fox Connor, who had been a mentor of both George Catlett Marshall and Dwight D. Eisenhower. Whatever this service did for Brown's professional development, it also seems to have expanded his self-image to the point that almost everyone who became acquainted with him in the 9th Infantry Division found the man insufferable. Major Tucker, undoubtedly the person who knew him best, has characterized Brown as:

> *Admirable in some hidden ways, liked by a few, tolerated and disliked by more. Arrogant, sophisticated, opinionated, difficult, snobbish, superior, demanding, interesting, concerned and courtly. A bachelor, never married; an enigma.*

Brown was the executive officer of the 39th when it shipped out of Fort Bragg ahead of other units involved with the invasion of Africa. The regiment went to Great Britain where it teamed up with the British-American task force that on November 8th, 1942, would assault Algiers, the easternmost objective of Operation Torch. One of the immediate results of that success, carried out under the watchful eyes of Eisenhower's staff, was promotion of the 39th's commander to brigadier general. When that officer was reassigned, Brown was promoted to colonel and given command. It is doubtful if this action was referred to General Eddy who, at this hour, was loading up what remained of this command at Fort Bragg for shipment to Casablanca.

The 39th Infantry and its parent Division did not link up until the eve of the Battle of El Guettar and in the course of this action the regiment's commander was affronted by Eddy's penchant for committing and directing the 39th's battalions on either flank of the 9th's attack. This finally led to an angry outburst from Brown in the presence of his S3, Major Tucker, who was surprised that Eddy did not relieve Brown of his command forthwith. The general did not take that action but relations between the two men soured. "I don't believe either trusted the other after that," Tucker observes.

This was the background then for a series of moves and countermoves on the part of 39th elements prior to D-Day as the regimental commander attempted to get them into the best position from which to attack, and the commanding general, worried about tipping his hand to the enemy, would at first agree to the moves and then cancel what Brown wished to do. For example, the 39th had most of its lst Battalion (Lt. Colonel Charles H. Cheatham) occupying Djebel el Hamra on April 19th. It was then moved back to its original position on Djebel el Oumela and then moved again on the 20th to positions on Rhonid el Hamra. At the same time the 2nd Battalion (Major Robert B. Cobb) occupied Djebel Garcia.

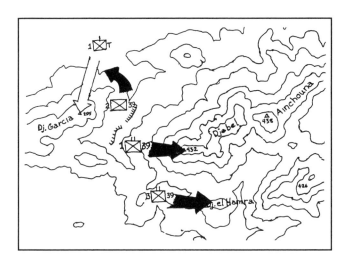

Map 4. 9th Infantry attack and counterattack.

Finally, on the night of April 22nd, the lst and 3rd Battalions (Lt. Colonel John T. Keeley) moved to a line of departure at the base of Hill 432 (Little Ainchouna) and Hill 280 (Djebel Fedjel) and the 2nd Battalion, in reserve, moved to an area on the eastern slope of Djebel Garcia.

The 39th's attack was to jump off at 0530 hours, April 23rd. The morning was foggy as usual and, there being no artillery preparation in hope of achieving surprise, it was very quiet. Brown proceeded to his observation post on the summit of Djebel Garcia with Tucker, his S3, and the commander of his reserve, Major Cobb. They occupied foxholes and waited. Then Cobb heard Brown ask Tucker for their copy of the division's field order. He says Tucker gave it to the colonel and then turned to go back to his hole. That is when Tucker indicated that he saw the Germans, Cobb recalls.

Major Tucker's recollection:

At first I was looking at Captain Felix Settlemire of Cannon Company and his OP party who were approaching. Then Settlemire stopped short and stared and I saw what had startled him. A number of German soldiers were even closer to us than he was. I yelled to the others, pulled my pistol and started firing. Brown and Cobb began firing too. Cobb fielded a potato masher grenade that flew in and tossed it back. But it was no use. They were all over us in a minute or two.

> *The Germans were from the Tunis 1 Battalion, part of the Manteuffel Division. They searched us, took watches and I lost my Citadel class ring. A non-com told several to take us back to their rear and he left with the others to join their unit which appeared to be headed east. Our guards marched us off to the north.*

Cobb:

> *It wasn't long before help was coming from F and G Companies of my battalion. They must have heard the exchange of fire and the grenades and figured out what had happened."*

Tucker:

> *Settlemire had circled around and had the first GIs he found attack the crest of Garcia. When they started firing we prisoners jumped our guards and dashed off to the west, finally ending up back with our own troops. Cobb was slightly wounded in this exchange. We learned later that this was a company-size combat patrol whose target was the 26th Field Artillery positions to our rear. The raiders were pretty much annihilated and I doubt if any made it back home.*

Captain George A. Pedrick, S1 of the Falcon 2nd Battalion, recalls:

> *Just before the attack was to jump off on the 23rd we at the CP heard a lot of firing from the vicinity of the OP. Major Herman, the executive officer, directed me to gather up what men were available and check it out. We had only started forward when we met Colonel Brown and the OP party returning. The Colonel was really shaken. He wanted to know which unit had effected his rescue. Someone said it was F Company. He told me that every man in that company was to get a medal for heroism. He was relieved before that action could go very far.*
>
> *I understand that a German patrol got through our lines and was on its way home when it came across Colonel Brown and his party at the OP. F Company was in position on the east side of the hill ready to jump off in the attack. I heard that the operations plan was lost to the Germans, and recall talk that, regardless of this loss, it was too late to make changes. The attack would proceed as planned.*

The enemy force on Djebel Garcia numbered about 150 men and lost 45 killed and a number of others taken prisoner in this action according to the official U.S. Army history of the African campaign.[1]

Pfc. Raymond J. Nichols of E Company, got one of the Germans:

> *Early on the morning of April 23rd our company came under attack from the rear as we were waiting for our own attack to jump off. When the Germans closed, one of them jumped up yelling 'Kamerade!' The company commander wanted to take him prisoner but I urged him to wait until we were sure it wasn't a trick. He stood up anyway. The German had a grenade behind his back and threw it. The explosion killed the captain and we killed the German.*

Sergeant Willard C. Hayes, a rifle squad leader of G Company, recollects:

> *On April 23rd we were in reserve behind the other companies attacking Djebel Ainchouna. Unknown to us a German patrol was behind our lines but we were alert. Suddenly I saw four Germans walking across a little hill about 40 yards away. I couldn't get the attention of my men without alerting the Germans and they were too far to throw a grenade. I waited until they came within 10 yards and stopped behind a big bush. Then I fired a full clip into that bush. There was quiet for a second and then all hell broke loose. Their bullets were hitting my pack and I tried to back away but was hit in the back and in the foot. My legs began to stiffen and I could feel hot blood running down the crack of my ass. One of my men cried out that he was hit and died very quickly. I was in pain but mostly worried about the Germans. I laid my head down on my rifle and pretended to be a goner. There was a sound of bushes moving and then a boot came down by my face. It was no GI shoe. When the German stepped over me, I turned my head and could see Private Tully on his knees with his back to us looking away. The German quickly grabbed Tully's rifle and stepped in front bringing up his rifle on Tully who was rising to his feet. I had time for one shot over Tully's shoulder. Without aiming, I hit the German over his right eye. His cap flew off and he died instantly.*
>
> *Tully went into shock and made a lot of noise. The other squad members came and a medic started to patch me up. Someone checked out the bush and found a dead German captain with eight bullet holes in him. The rest of his party must have taken off.*

For all of the excitement going on behind the 39th's line of departure H-hour saw its assault units moving forward against opposition that was easily overcome. The first day's objectives were taken by

1400 hours. Then the 1st Battalion was ordered to continue its advance along the spine of Djebel Ainchouna to take Hill 438. The 3rd Battalion, having taken Djebel Hamra without opposition, was ordered to leave one company to secure it and to join the 1st Battalion on Ainchouna.

Because of a dense scrub growth found between Djebels Hamra and Ainchouna, the 3rd Battalion was unable to close on the 1st before darkness. The 1st had run into stiffened opposition on Hill 438 and was unable to take it.

1st Lieutenant Stanford L. Downs of C Company recalls:

> *C Company attacked up the western slope of Little Ainchouna in skirmish formation. As we approached the crest we were in open timber and came under heavy rifle, machine gun and artillery fire. elements of the company flanked to the right and hit the German positions from the south. Under this pressure, the enemy withdrew and joined others on the westernmost of the two peaks which dominated the ridge. We pursued and dug in for the night in close contact with the enemy. We had been in several fire fights during the day and on one occasion we had exchanged grenades. We had a number of casualties.*

Pfc. Gene Magidson was one of them. The C Company riflemen recollects:

> *I was lucky when wounded on April 23rd. I was about to throw a grenade and had not yet pulled the pin when I was shot. The bullet shattered my shoulder and collarbone, and I felt like I'd been hit with a baseball bat, but that would have been the least of my troubles if I'd gotten that pin pulled. My buddies took good care of me, even taking down my pants so I could go. I had to wait eight hours before I could be evacuated.*

Another knocked out early in the game was Pfc. Thomas J. Boyle, radio operator from the 26th Field Artillery Battalion:

> *My stay in the Sedjenane valley did not last long. Our forward observer party started along a road to contact the 3rd Battalion of the 39th. When we reached a small rise in the road, Lieutenant Craig and Sergeant Elmer Fowler went ahead on foot to reconnoiter. They were only out of sight when my good buddy, Gilbert Meyer from Wisconsin, and I came under mortar attack and both of us were wounded. We managed to move back a short distance and met soldiers from 9th Recon. Later we were evacuated and I rejoined the 26th at Magenta to learn that Craig and Fowler had been taken prisoner by the Germans that day.*

Shortly before midnight on April 23rd, General Stroh, the 9th's assistant division commander, arrived at the regiment's command post and, in private, formally relieved Colonel Brown of his command.[2] Brown had his bags and bedroll packed quickly and was gone. Stroh conferred with Lt. Colonel Van H. Bond, the executive officer, and Tucker. He made no changes in plans made by Brown for continuing the attack in the morning. The 2nd Battalion, still in reserve, was ordered to relieve the company of the 3rd Battalion which had been left to secure Djebel Hamra. Then the general returned to the division command post. Bond and Tucker could only shake their heads and return to sweating out what was going on up front.

lst Lieutenant Chester Braune, Jr., General Stroh's aide de camp (ADC), remembers:

In connection with Colonel Brown's capture I heard many rumors about missing orders and a situation map but Generals Eddy and Stroh did not attach much important to that, or the fact that he'd been captured. Most of their concern centered on what they perceived as poor morale in the 39th. This was the primary reason for his being relieved. As for Stroh's command of the 39th for those few days before a replacement could be brought in, we went up each day and he ran the show. Then, when things were buttoned up, he'd turn things over to Bond, the executive officer, and we'd return to the 9th CP.

One incident that occurred when moving back and forth gives some insight into the character of the general. We were driving across a field following the tracks of previous traffic when we came upon a weapons carrier which had just hit a mine. There was nothing to be done. Stroh told the driver to pull around the wreck and continue. I admit my knuckles were white as we did so.

Major Frank L. Gunn, executive officer of the 3rd Battalion, comments:

I don't know that the 39th's morale was any poorer or better than that of any other unit of the division. Furthermore, I don't think that Colonel Brown's relief had any appreciable effect on the regiment's performance.

Whatever the morale of the rest of the regiment, that of the lst Battalion was to sustain a major blow on the morning of April 24th. 2nd Lieutenant Jack A. Dunlap of B Company recalls:

We continued the attack on the 23rd past the crest of Little Ainchouna, eliminating several machine gun nests along the way.

We then reorganized for the final assault on Big Ainchouna. Captain Fuller, my company commander, directed me to take my platoon and deploy in a skirmish line along the side of the objective. When the entire company was similarly deployed, he would give the order to attack the crest.

By the time my platoon was deployed it was late afternoon. We laid there on that steep slope waiting for orders but nothing happened. Meanwhile the Germans threw in a number of artillery preparations where I had last seen Captain Fuller and the CP personnel.

We waited there the rest of the night with no further word on the attack. The Krauts pummeled us with some kind of heavy artillery, a round every fifteen minutes or so. At daylight I crawled over to where I'd seen Fuller and found chaos. The commander had been wounded and evacuated. The first sergeant was laying under a tree, dead. About half of our mortar section were casualties. The company executive officer wasn't functioning and would not assume command. Another platoon leader had an eye knocked out of focus and he went down the hill seeking medical attention. After checking around I determined that I was the only officer left in the company. Never before or since have I felt so forlorn or inadequate.

I reorganized the company as best I could. There were 54 men left, most from my platoon. I moved them to cover and then set out to find the Battalion CO and report on B Company.

Soon I found a sergeant from battalion headquarters who told me that Big Ainchouna had been taken by C Company. He said the battalion commander was just 500 yards ahead and he showed me our commo wire to follow.

Clouds or fog were with us again that morning. The atmosphere was damp and chilly but, when I found Colonel Cheatham and his staff, I began to feel better. They were in an open area, gathered in a semicircle about a spread-out map. I reported on B Company's situation and the colonel told me to wait for orders. I walked away behind some large boulders and sat down for a smoke.

By the time I finished my cigarette the clouds had started to lift. A few minutes later sunlight broke through and then four or five fast rounds of direct fire artillery, probably 88s, came in among the gathered staff with devastating accuracy. Colonel Cheatham suffered a concussion and his executive officer, Major Ratteree, was killed instantly by a massive head wound. The S2 was also dead. Captain Beale lost an arm and died later. If the

German weapon had been high trajectory, the staff group could have heard it and taken cover. Major Ratteree was killed in the kneeling position. I was directed to bring B Company to join the rest of the Battalion on Big Ainchouna. It was here that I learned that Captain Anderson, CO of C Company had assumed command of the Battalion. He did an outstanding job during this critical period and in leading us on our subsequent missions.

Again, lst Lieutenant Stanford L. Downs of C Company:

At dawn the 2nd morning the battlefield was covered by a dense fog. I went out alone and reconnoitered the terrain between our positions and the crest of Hill 438. The Germans had pulled out. I found Captain Beall, D Company commander, out there doing the same thing, also by himself. After a short discussion we went our separate ways. The fog lifted rather suddenly just as I returned and I heard a salvo of four or five artillery rounds explode to our right flank. Captain Beall was caught in the open and killed. Later on I learned that the same fire had decimated the battalion command group. Captain Anderson, our CO, took over the battalion and put me in charge of the company after first relieving all of the other officers for their lack of leadership.

1st Lieutenant Charles Scheffel of A Company, was another witness to the debacle of the lst Battalion command group:

At dawn on the 24th there was drizzle. Low clouds and fog enveloped us. We had no orders and, as A Company's commander was absent, I decided to go to the battalion command post to find out what was happening. I stayed on the ridge back the way we had come the night before and soon found Colonel Cheatham and his staff in a huddle in an open space surrounded by huge boulders. The Colonel asked our situation. After I told him he said to wait among the boulders for orders. About that time some patches of sunlight hit the area. The fog was lifting. Then an in-coming shell hit square in the middle of the officers' meeting. More shells followed quickly.

Nearly everyone of the command group was killed or wounded. For a while confusion reigned but then Captain Anderson appeared and, after a few questions, he allowed that since he was the senior officer remaining in the battalion, he was taking command. I decided to return to the company and get it ready to move.

Soon after I got back to the company the Germans hit us.

Fortunately we were alert and had spent the time while waiting for orders improving our positions on commanding ground. We dealt a lot of damage to the enemy. I counted 25 bodies when we moved out the next morning.

Sergeant William M. Kreye, intelligence sergeant of the lst Battaion, wrote after the war about the incident, adding a few details to what happened on Big Ainchouna:[3]

All of us were advancing along the plateau. A very heavy mist presided on the hill. The mist began to lift and we were suddenly pinned down by the cross-fire of two rapid-firing weapons. Bill Solliday and yours truly took cover in a slight draw on the southern side of the ridge. Caban and Mati were in a similar draw just a few yards ahead of us. The rest of the personnel of the CP were up above us on the plateau and everyone was trying to find and take cover.

To the south of the valley a German 105mm self-propelled gun started to pump shells at us. I heard the report of the gun and the bursts of the shells at precisely the same time. It was hair-raising. The effect of this action caused casualties by the score. Major Ratteree, Captain Beall and Lieutenant Stanton were killed. Other casualties were Colonel Cheatham, Captain Terrell and many others.

Speaking for myself, and I believe as well for Mati, Caban and Solliday, I didn't worry too much about the small arms fire as we seemed to have, momentarily, protection from the cross-fire of the machine guns. But this gun action was something else. Then, after minutes that seemed like hours, the gun stopped firing. The German infantry started to counterattack along the plateau. Mati and Caban had the British 46 radio in their possession. One or both opened up on the frequency of the 26th Field Artillery. They gave the location of our positions. The first volleys of the American shells landed into the onrushing Germans.

'Cease fire! Cease fire!' Caban or Mati shouted into the radio. The next burst, if it had come, might have blown us off of that hill. The Germans changed their minds after that and withdrew. Mati and Caban had saved the day; they saved the whole operation.

Pfc. Raymond J Nichols of E Company recalls:

We attacked a large, heavily wooded mountain but there were no Germans so our CO asked for a round of smoke on the objective. It popped on the next mountain to the east so we knew we were on the wrong one. The next day we moved to the mountain where the smoke had lit and found the Germans waiting for us. By now we had a new CO, Captain Preston O. Gordon. He was a great commander.

Staff Sergeant Albert "Hawk" DiRisio, mess sergeant of B Company, 39th Infantry, recalls:

I was leading my 'safari porters' of kitchen personnel each carrying a case of C-rations or a 5-gallon water can, through the high brush. We had the troops' Easter meal. It was a warm sunny day and I was just thinking we should have arrived at the company position when Charlie Schlegel, behind me, tapped me on the shoulder and signalled to be quiet. Then, I could hear Germans talking just ahead. They had not detected us. I set down my water can and signalled the others to do the same, quietly, and to reverse tracks.

The further we made it out of there the faster we moved until, coming to an open area, I found myself facing Sergeant Pat Jerome and B Company's machine guns. 'Jesus Christ, Hawk!' he hollered. 'How come you're coming from that direction?'

The company was going to attack the next morning and I told the hungry men they were going to have to fight for their rations. Sure enough, soon after they jumped off, they found the rations where we had left them. They also found an abandoned German tank which the Germans had out there. I guess we made the right decision not to take them on.

Lt. Colonel Keeley's 3rd Battalion. took up the lead of the Falcons following the German's counterattack on April 24th and cleared the eastern end of Djebel Ainchouna. It had become obvious, however, that the 51-year old Keeley was breaking. His executive officer, Major Frank L. Gunn, had been wounded and evacuated and now the entire burden of command, as well as the physical exertions demanded by the rough terrain, were wearing the commander down.

2nd Lieutenant George I. Connolly, his observer from the 34th Field Artillery, notes:

Keeley was shaky. He was too old to be an infantry battalion commander out here. Gunn, the 'fire' of the battalion, was gone. When we reached Ainchouna's eastern end, Keeley requested fire down into the valley to the east where Germans reportedly had been gathered. I pinpointed the place by one of those white-washed Arab gravesites but could see no enemy. An officer from

one of the rifle companies came up and told me that he had a
patrol in the target area and I reported this to Keeley. He
insisted that we fire the mission and we did, half white phospho-
rus and half high explosive. The shells were still bursting when
we spotted GIs running back out of the smoke. Keeley then came
running over to me--- 'Cease fire! Add 100!' The GIs returned
with specks of the chemical having charred their clothes.

In the meantime, the 39th's lst Battalion was gravitating to the
northeast and the 2nd Battalion occupied without opposition Hill 498
to the south. For three days, General Stroh had been the 39th's commander but, in the opinion of Major Tucker, the Falcon's executive
officer, Lt. Colonel Van H. Bond, "was the glue which held things
together." Colonel William L. Ritter reported on April 27th and took
command of the regiment. It wasn't long after that when Keeley broke
down completely and had to be evacuated. Bond was given command
of the battalion.

By this time it was apparent that the 3rd Battalion of the Corps
Franc d'Afrique, was not able to maintain a place on the northern
flank of the 39th. This led to the move of the Falcon's lst Battalion to
Hill 164, and from there to the final hills dominating the 9th Division's
objective, the junction where the road from Jefna joined the
Mateur-Bizerte highway. While this was going on, more attention was
focused on the 39th's advance to the southeast where observation on
exits from Jefna promised a break in the German defense facing the
47th Infantry.

lst Lieutenant William J. Butler, medical officer of A Company,
9th Medical Battalion, has written about medical support of the 9th's
attack at this time:[4]

The casualty evacuation proved to be far more efficient in II
Corps under General Bradley (notwithstanding the more difficult
terrain of northern Tunisia). The evacuation hospital wasn't 50
miles to the Division's rear, large numbers of casualties didn't
pile up in the Division, and things seemed far more organized
and businesslike. There appeared to be emphasis on efficient
care and evacuation of casualties to maintain morale.

The enemy suddenly pulled out on May 1st and Company A
moved forward to an open hill within sight of Djebel Ichkeul.
From there I could see where the road from Jefna forked one
way to Mateur and the other way to Bizerte. On May 3rd we
watched the 1st Armored Division's attack on Mateur from there.
Our air superiority had been a comfort during the battle. We had
watched the Luftwaffe bomb Mateur two days earlier, but when

they attacked yesterday they found the heavy flak there too much for them.

Again, lst Lieutenant Jack A. Dunlap of B Company:

> *Back in these days before penicillin we were given big sulpha pills for the wounded to swallow. When we ran out of water, the best we could do was crush the pills and sprinkle the powder directly on the wound. When we finally got water it came in former gas tins that hadn't been cleaned so we were getting about ten percent high octane. Bad-tasting stuff to a cotton-mouthed, split-lip SOB like myself.*

lst Lieutenant Philip T. Lones, executive officer of the Falcon's Cannon Company, remembers:

> *It was in the vicinity of Djebel Ainchouna. Our guns were well-sited behind us, ready for immediate action. My team was back on the reverse slope and I was forward on the grassy, gently rounded top of a high ridge. I had been squinting through my field glasses for several hours, all the while keeping an eye on an Arab goatherd who was tending his flock a few hundred yards to my right.*
>
> *Becoming hungry I opened a C-ration and, emptying some water into my canteen cup, I heated it and dumped in the bitter powdered coffee from the ration. Just as I was about to take a sip, the Arab goatherd started running towards me, shouting something like 'Non! Non!' I was relieved to see he was unarmed and merely wanted to get my attention. He motioned that I was to hand over the cup and, curious, I did so. He then hurried over to one of his nearby goats and squeezed some warm milk into the coffee and returned it with a big smile.*
>
> *How was this fellow to know that I preferred milk in my coffee, even goat milk? Quickly dismissing any thought of contamination, I drank the tasty drink and profusely thanked my kind 'neighbor' who, by the way, would accept no food or other reward. I have never forgotten this good guy and his most welcome gesture.*

Major Robert B. Cobb, commanding officer of the 2nd Battalion:

> *Regarding General Stroh's command of the regiment I would rate him as one of the most caring and knowledgeable infantry leaders the 9th Division had. After he took over he came up every day to help me carry out orders and listen to my concerns. Then, when Colonel Ritter took over I found him equally willing to listen. Though not as technically proficient, perhaps,*

as other commanders, due to his long service with another branch, he was constantly up with us and available to talk to. For example, on April 27th, in the course of our attack on Hill 382, which had been closely coordinated with Divarty, our lead company was badly shot up by enemy fire and its commander was killed. I sought permission to hold up the attack until we could replace that company and Colonel Ritter did not hestitate to agree and he delayed those supporting fires. When we moved out again, the Germans had backed off and Hill 382 was easily and quickly taken. It provided observation of Jefna and the road east from there to Mateur. Now the Germans had to get out of their Green-Bald Hill positions.

General Stroh's colored map clearly showed that attainment of Hill 406 was finally going to open the way down from the overgrown, roadless upland that the 39th had been tied up in for a week. But if the consequences of getting there were apparent to the Americans, they were fully as appreciated by the enemy. Prisoners confirmed that this dominant feature had been designated as critical terrain, to be defended to the last man. Accordingly, Colonel Ritter, the Falcons' new leader, began early to plan a careful, coordinated approach to this position and its assault.

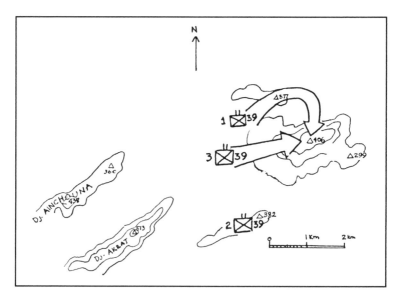

Map 5. 39th Infantry attacks Hill 406, 30 April 1943.

-88-

The tactics for Hill 406 were simple. One battalion, the 3rd of Lt. Colonel Bond, would approach it directly from the west over a long, open, gently rising course. The Americans figured that, as the hills ran out with this feature, the Germans would depart from their favorite reverse slope defense and put almost everything up front, taking full advantage of those excellent fields of fire. It was deemed likely that the 3rd Battalion's approach would fix the defenders attention and they would fail to detect a wide covered swing around the north flank by Captain Anderson's lst Battalion.

Because of the 60th's progress to the east even further north, Anderson's route would probably be empty of the enemy and the lst Battalion might approach Hill 406 from the rear undetected. It would face a mean climb up the sharp eastern face of that feature but, if Jerry had everything up front watching the 3rd Battalion, their scaling might be unopposed.

The keys to unlocking this tactical problem were first, to carefully plan artillery support to provide overwhelming countermeasures to German firepower as it was uncovered; next, speed on the lst Battalion's part in its sweep around the left; finally, a crushing mass of firepower to be delivered in the final assault of the position. Ritter and his staff, Bond and Anderson, and their artillery advisers carefully and repeatedly went over the simple but daring plan, making certain that every available rifleman and supporting weapon would be brought into play. Patrols were ordered around the clock confirming what the map indicated and pinpointing enemy dispositions as well as other targets. One full day, the 29th, was taken up in preparation for what the 9th Division's after-action report would describe as "one of the turning points for the entire campaign."[5] The report's April 30th entry laconically describes how, indeed, "battle is the pay-off":

> *The attack of the 39th Infantry on Hill 406 on this date was completely successful. One battalion occupied this hill, and one pushed forward to the east as far as Spur 299, leaving one battalion on Hill 382. This area completely dominated the complicated terrain just to the south, as well as the road leading northeast toward the head of the Sedjenane valley. It was evidently in this area that the Germans had concentrated many of their supply dumps and other installations for the support of their Green-Bald Hill positions. With the dominant observation in our possession, effective shelling of these installations was possible. In a single day the 26th Field Artillery Battalion fired over 4,000 rounds with devastating effect. The main German defenses had now been outflanked and, the next day, their withdrawal to the northeast began.*

2nd Lieutenant George I. Connolly of the 34th Field Artillery Battalion remembers some of that shooting:

After a break of several days I went back to the 39th Infantry just after they had taken Hill 406 in such spectacular fashion. It had a long, unobstructed approach on the west side. You wondered, if there was a defense, how anyone crossed it alive. Happily, Jerry's head was down due to the preparatory fires. While this was going on, the main effort came on the position from the rear, up an almost 90-degree slope. That broke their backs. On reaching the top there was complete observation all the way to Mateur. I was told that the 26th's forward observer really did catch them down in the valley when he got up there.

I put an OP in the saddle between the main peak and the spur. Someone gave me a rifle squad for security and I had a field day shooting. Coincidently, I took two prisoners from that OP. One was still completely shell-shocked from the artillery preparation laid down for the assault. The other was a Pole who had only been in Tunisia for a few days. He said that his whole thought since landing was to find someone to take him in.

lst Lieutenant Stanford L. Downs of C Company summarizes the Djebel Ainchouna operation and its aftermath:

The 1st Battalion pushed eastward from djebel to djebel. None of these hills were strongly defended but fire fights with small groups of defenders were common. Some enemy units surrendered without a fight; others defended briefly and then withdrew before we could close on them. We were frequently under artillery bombardment or long-range small arms from hills other than the objective. We took casualties. Throughout this interval we maintained our assigned schedule and captured all objectives in a timely manner.

Capture of that last ridgeline before the Mateur plains completed the drive through the mountainous terrain and was our most noteworthy action following our taking Ainchouna. We approached from the north and, despite a brief but spirited defense by a small German unit at the mountain's base, and long-range rifle and machine gun fire from a hill to our left rear, we quickly seized the crest of Hill 406.

In the valley to the south a dirt road ran parallel to the ridge line. The Germans had obviously expected our advance on this road and prepared an ambush from well dug-in positions on the steep south face of the ridge. Fortunately for us they weren't occupied when we came along.

On May 6th the 39th moved onto the Mateur plain and was attached to the lst Armored Division. Lt. Colonel Keeley was relieved for exhaustion and Major Harry C. Herman assumed command of the 3rd Battalion.

Notes

1. Howe, *Northwest Africa,* p. 618.

2. Colonel Brown was ultimately reduced a grade by administrative action of a higher headquarters. He was then reassigned to the 36th Infantry Division in Italy and, while commanding a battalion in action there, he was awarded the Silver Star Medal for heroism. Subsequently returned to the U.S., Brown again was promoted to colonel while serving at Fort Benning.

It is suggested in the Division history, *Eight Stars to Victory,* that plans for the 9th Division's attack were lost in the process of Brown's capture. Major Tucker states that the division's plans were not taken to the OP; that what Brown had asked him for at the OP was a map with the battalion's positions plotted, but this map was never turned over to the enemy. It was destroyed. It is perhaps significant that while Major Cobb recalls being questioned on this point by an investigator for Brown's board, Tucker maintains that he was never asked by anyone to give his recollection of the events.

3. William N. Kreye, *The Pawns of War,* pp. 116-117. Available from Greater New York Chapter, 9th Inf. Div. Assn., c/o Art Schmidt, 69-20 69th St., Glendale NY 11385-6696.

4. William J. Butler, *Boondock,* p. 35. (Unfinished manuscript in the author's file, or write to Dr. Butler at 3327 Lakehill Dr., Kalamazoo, MI, 49008.

5. *Report of Operation Conducted by 9th Infantry Division, 11 April-8 May 1943,* p. 12.

60th Infantry patrol north of Lake Ichkeul, 7 May 1943.
(Army Signal Corps photo.)

Dune Vaillance Admirable

GO DEVILS GO

The field telephone buzzed briefly in the hauptmann's ear and awoke him:

'Prahast hier,' he grunted.

'Sie kommen,' said the voice at the other end of the line and it went on to explain that two, perhaps three, battalions of American infantry were on the move, headed for the Djebel Dardyss positions just vacated by the 2nd Battalion, 756th Mountain Regiment. The caller was the staff duty officer of the severely understrength 962nd Afrika Schuetzen Regiment which now had the responsibility for defending the entire 14-mile sector from the Mediterranean to the Jefna approach.[1]

Hauptmann Prahast, assistant Ia (operations officer) of the Division von Manteuffel, assured the duty officer that help would be forthcoming if the enemy entered the critical Djebel Dardyss position, and he immediately called the Division's reserve to get it started in that direction. There was no doubt in his mind that it would be needed.

It was uncanny, Prahast thought, how quickly the Amis reacted. At Division they had screamed their protests at losing the 756th Battalion but higher headquarters claimed the threat was even greater further south. As compensation, Division von Manteuffel was being augmented with two armored reconnaissance battalions but these were of little use in the hills. 'Maybe Witzig can produce another miracle,' the hauptmann concluded, 'but I doubt it.'

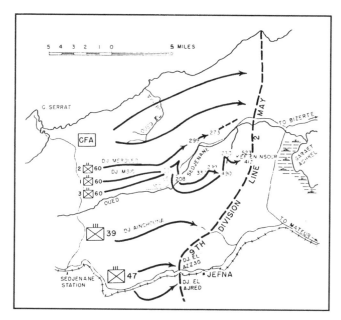

Map 6. Northern Area: 60th and Corps Franc d'Afrique.
(From To Bizerte with II Corps.*)*

Major Rudolf Witzig, 11th Parachute Engineer Battalion, wrote a 1991 account of his unit's WWII actions and in it recounts:[2]

> *On 24 April the battalion, having a strength of perhaps 150 men, is ordered to counterattack Djebel Dardyss which lies north of the Sedjenane river, about 12 kilometers northwest of the Jefna position. The enemy is American and much superior in numbers. We are repulsed and can disengage only by some ruse, walking out of the encirclement in indian file through dense brush.*

Among those whose advance disturbed the sleep of Manteuffel's operations officer and put Witzig's engineers in motion was an archtypical 60th Infantry soldier. Before the next day was done, however, Sergeant William L. Nelson, a mortar section leader of the regiment's H Company, would earn his nation's highest award for valor and die in battle. On this morning of April 23rd, though, the 25-year old Nelson trudged along in his column carrying an extra round of light high explosive ammunition for his mortars. It could have been loaded with the product of his old outfit in civilian life, Hercules Powder Company of Wilmington, Delaware. Nelson had landed a white-collar job at Hercules after completing a two-year program at Beacom Business College in Wilmington. There he met and became engaged to a fellow student, Rebecca Pyle. Nelson was inducted into the Army on January 9, 1941 and trained at nearby Fort Dix, New Jersey, ultimately joining the 60th Infantry at Fort Bragg, North Carolina. He came home on furlough and married Rebecca.

On D-Day of the 9th Division's attack in Northern Tunisia, one of the forward observers was also serving as an ammunition bearer because Major Michael B. Kauffman, commanding the 2nd Battalion, 60th Infantry, ordered that every enlisted man and officer who had a spare hand would carry an extra round of mortar ammunition. The battalion was taking to the bush where no vehicle could follow. Everything that might be needed for a fight had to be hand-carried forward and, since the 2nd was leading the regiment's advance, it was inevitable that in any fight the battalion would be on its own for a while. The walking reserve of mortar ammunition then would be invaluable.

After the war the late Reverend Ralton M. Speers, once sergeant major of the 1st Battalion, 60th Infantry, wrote of his unit's experiences in the Sedjenane valley.[3]

> *On 23 April the Battalion left the assembly area combat-loaded but without organic transportation due to the impassable terrain which we were to encounter. Mule trains were organized to carry heavy equipment and haul rations, also this would be the only method of evacuation. During 23 and 24 April, the organization reached and assembled on Djebel M'rata and, while the Battalion was there, the enemy shelled the area with artillery and mortar fire. During the period 25 to 30 April the Battalion moved along quite steadily, often under cover of darkness, over several ridges meeting with little enemy resistance. Those few enemy that were met were rear guard outposts.*

Among veterans of the 9th Infantry Division of World War II, Lt. Colonel (Ret.) Matt Urban is a living legend. In 1980, thirty-five years after events in Normandy covered in his citation, Urban was invited to the White House by President Jimmy Carter and decorated with the Medal of Honor. But on April 23rd, 1943, while commanding F Company, 60th Infantry, 1st Lieutenant Matty Urbanowitz, as he was then known, was cutting his teeth as a hero, showing the ferocity and dedication that were his hallmark. In his autobiography, Urban describes his unit's part in seizing Djebel M'rata.[4]

> *By luck or 'Hand of God' the attackers had penetrated into the foothills where the vegetation diminished as they reached the edge of the slope. There was enough cover for concealment yet the ground allowed for maneuverability. By late afternoon the exhausted troops reached the jump-off point. They rested in seclusion at the edge of the jungle.*
>
> *Here they shed canteens. They secured bayonets on their M1*

rifles. A tense and total silence accompanied last minute preparations. The faint sound of laughter drifted over the rise. The German troops were completely unaware of the impending attack. 'These guys aren't even looking,' Urban thought to himself. 'They're goofing off.' Fear and excitement marked the faces of the men around him.

The soldiers of the Ninth were in a position below the enemy force that had held out against British commandos for months on end. Lieutenant Urban moved up and down the jump-off point. He was double checking to see that all equipment was secured so no metal would clank nor any sun-reflected surface would signal their approach. All communication was reduced to hand signals. Dirt was rubbed onto sweaty faces. The attack force was ready for its 'Big Jump.'

With a flare gun in one hand and a .45 in the other, Urban crept a few yards in front. He fired the flare along a flat trajectory. This dropped the torch-like shell smack in the middle of a German machine gun nest. Men scattered in every direction. Some enemy soldiers gaped in frozen amazement as the next volley of burning phosphorous exploded. It showered the perimeter of the machine gun nest with streaks of dreaded luminous red fire. Urban lobbed another cartridge with his improvised 'miniature flame thrower,' if only to demoralize the enemy.

At Urban's signal the troops of F Company, 60th Infantry, moved forward and burst over the gun emplacement before the bewildered German defenders realized what was happening.

1st Sergeant John W. Miller of F Company does not recall his unit's response to Lieutenant Urbanowitz' call to advance as being so spontaneous:

When Matty yelled 'Charge!' no one moved. The commander was furious and called together the officers and senior NCOs: 'Sergeant Miller will follow up with his Tommy gun ready and he's to shoot any SOB who doesn't move. Go tell 'em!'

After a minute or two, Matty yelled again and this time no one faltered. There was a little resistance from the Germans but most ran off. We had a couple of men men killed by their return fire.

Sergeant Schwachter of the 5th Kompanie, 962nd Afrika Schuetzen Regiment, later reported of the attack of Djebel M'rata:[5]

American troops whose lines lay between one and five miles distant from our own crossed a minefield in 'No Man's Land' to begin their attack on 25 (sic) April. They went to ground under our fire but under a well-coordinated barrage they soon worked their way to within hand grenade range. My platoon covered the withdrawal of our battalion to higher ground and was heavily engaged. We had heavy losses because my men had no recent combat experience. One 42-year-old man who had been convicted of treason and who had helped beat back the American assaults, said to me, 'Sergeant, I don't care what happens now. I have redeemed my honor.' and another man stood up in his slit trench firing a machine gun from the hip and driving back the advancing Americans until he was wounded.

Major Kauffman's first day objective was Djebel M'rata, 11,500 yards due east of his Battalion's start point. Even before the attack began the major worried about M'rata's domination by Djebel Dardyss, not 1,000 yards southeast and obviously higher than the objective.

"They'll be looking down our throats from there," Kauffman pointed out to his commander, Colonel de Rohan. Even then the 60th's intelligence officer had an enemy battalion plotted in positions on Dardyss. "They know the ground better than we do," the Major argued, "and, if they're there, it's because Dardyss is the commanding territory."

DeRohan allowed that if the Germans were still entrenched on Dardyss in strength, that made a solid case for stopping short on M'rata and getting set before proceeding. "Keep your scouts out," he cautioned.

Technical Sergeant Charles S. Willsher, sergeant major of the 60th's 3rd Battalion, entered in his journal:[6]

23 April. The Battalion CO (Major John H. Dilley) reported to regimental headquarters at 0530 and returned at 0700 to move the battalion one mile east and then returned to regiment to await orders. He received orders to send patrols north. The patrols had not returned when the battalion was ordered to move at 1230 to J335906 (north end of Djebel M'rata.) The battalion completed the move and the CO reported to the regimental commander that the battalion was on line as ordered. Wires were laid and pack mules began to supply the battalion. Orders were received after dark to move forward the following morning to capture hills at J371890 and J361876.

24 April. The battalion moved at daylight to J356900. There was no resistance and seven political prisoners were taken.[7] (Major Dilley) noticed enemy activity in the valley at J386908, consisting of trucks, tanks and artillery. (Major Dilley) and other officers directed artillery fire at the enemy positions. The enemy had been firing on the 2nd Battalion on the right. (Major Dilley) saw that Companies K and L took up positions along the ridges, and reported to regimental headquarters on the situation. He was instructed to hold present positions and to attack at 0800 in the morning. The 3rd Battalion-directed artilley fire had resulted in considerable withdrawal of enemy units in the valley.

Major Michael B. Kauffman, commanding the 2nd Battalion, 60th Infantry recalls:

Our original objective was Djebel M'rata but, when we got there, after a fight, I saw that Djebel Dardyss dominated the area as much as I had anticipated it would so I ordered the battalion to continue.

Later, Major Kauffman contributed to the regiment's annual historical report. Describing events of April 24th, he wrote:[8]

The next morning, April 24th, brought that eventful day that will never be forgotten by members of the battalion who were there. The battalion was deployed with 'E' on the left, 'F' in the center and 'G' on the right. H Company's mortars were in positions in rear supporting the battalion.

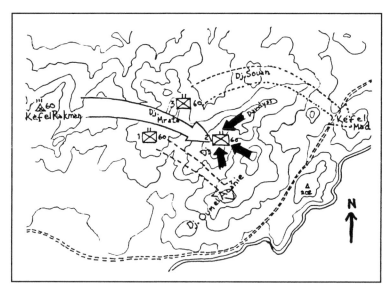

Map 7. Defense of Djebel Dardyss.

The morning was very foggy and observation was difficult. At about 0745 the Jerries counterattacked our position. It was estimated, and substantiated by prisoners later, that approximately two reinforced German battalions attacked. Our boys opened up on them with everything we had and mowed down many of the attackers. This did not stop the Jerries, however, because they had orders to take the hill at all costs. They continually attacked from everywhere and, even though the battalion had no artillery support whatsoever, the defense was so organized that Jerry could not penetrate it.

At this stage of the game there was a little humor brought into the picture, although it was not considered funny at the time. You could see and hear members of the battalion as they would shout, 'They're coming from the right!' At this the reserve would run to the right flank to reinforce it and drive the Jerries back. Then someone would shout, 'They're coming from the left,' and the reserve would take off for the left flank. In this battle H Company's machine gunners, along with every man in the battalion, showed the type of American soldier that he is and proved that he was better than the Jerries. All during these four hours of counterattacking the battalion was constantly shelled by mortar and artillery fire but they stuck to their guns.

When the smoke cleared away the enemy had withdrawn leaving 116 dead and many more wounded and captured. This was indeed one of the most decided victories of the campaign and made possible the capture of Mateur. However great the victory, we had losses of gallant men, who we will always remember for their daring gallantry and bravery. Twenty-three of our men lay dead on the Djebel and 190 were wounded (later corrected to be 21 killed and 111 wounded). Despite these losses, morale of the Battalion was high and confidence in themselves later reinforced the men's ability to accomplish any task undertaken.

Immediately following his withdrawal the enemy pounded the position with mortar and artillery fire.

During the attack our ammunition was getting dangerously low and members of the staff with some men who were slightly wounded collected what ammunition was left on the dead and wounded and distributed it among the men on the front line. In fact, our ammunition supply became so low that men were using German guns and ammunition.

Because of the rapidity with which the battalion moved across the terrain and the distance travelled, the supply route was lengthened so far that it was very difficult to get supplies to the troops. When the battalion jumped off on the 23rd, they had in their possession two-thirds of a C-ration which lasted that day. All day on the 24th the men were without food and it wasn't until the night of the 25th that rations were brought up to the battalion by mule train. The mule train had difficulty locating the battalion and had been roaming the hills looking for us. Despite the absence of food and water, the men realized the difficulty of getting supplies and were patient until they could be brought up. The dead were evacuated from the Djebel by use of the mule train and taken back to the supply point.

Again, lst Sergeant Miller of F Company:

On Djebel Dardyss, Sergeant Joe Boylan, Bill Nichols and I took positions near the center of the company line. At about 0500 on the 24th all hell broke loose. Artillery and mortar shells were crashing down and we knew an attack would follow. As it got light enemy small arms began to fly. The first Germans I saw were of a machine gun squad which went into position only a few paces ahead of my hole. They had no idea I was there until I jumped up and cut loose with my submachine gun. When there was a lull I crawled out and brought in their gun and ammunition. I set it up and began to fire.

The Germans made a push every hour it seemed. One time on our front, the next to the right or left. German officers were yelling in English, 'Withdraw! Withdraw!' and Matty Urbanowitz would run up and yell, 'No! No! Hold your positions and fire!'

By that afternoon we were out of food and low on ammunition. I crawled out and searched the German bodies and got some help there. Deeper in the woods I could hear this pitiful cry, 'Hilfe! Hilfe!' I couldn't stand it so I found this German with a gaping thigh wound and carried him back to our position. Matty said I should have killed the SOB. I don't know why his own people didn't take care of him.

Pfc William H. Nichols of F Company remembers:

I remember Sergeant Miller's firing that MG34 and the German's trick of sending forward a man with a white flag and then blasting any of our boys who stood up to receive him.

Perhaps because of their few numbers Delawareans seem to be more tightly connected than the populations of other states. They appear to care more about one another, or at least they did 50 years ago. Then, after the bad news of Pearl Harbor and the debacle at Kasserine Pass, news of the heroism of a local boy and a victory in far-off

Tunisia was popularly gratifying. News of Bill Nelson's sacrifice was taken up as "family business" throughout the state. When it came time to do the honors, many got into the act.

Franklin M. Reck was a professional writer who decided to do a book about the nation's first 18 winners of the Medal of Honor in World War II and this would include the former 60th Infantry mortarman. In the winter of 1944 Reck's research took him to Carlisle, Pennsylvania, to interview Major John H. Dilley, a student there at the Army War College. Reck later wrote to Nelson's widow, Rebecca, of his conversation with the former commander of the Go Devil's 3rd Battalion:[9]

> *They (60th Infantry) went into position in the hills north of the town of Sedjenane. The plan for the 23rd (of April, 1943) was for the 2nd Battalion to lead the attack. The objective for that first day was a point halfway along a high ridge known as Djebel Dardyss. They made this objective against considerable opposition and that night they were sleeping among the rocks and brush of Djebel Dardyss. That night the 1st Battalion came up on the right of the 2nd and the 3rd Battalion moved into line on the left, closer to the Mediterranean coast. Now the whole regiment was on line, with your husband's battalion in the center on the hill.*
>
> *The Germans had to do something to stop this advance and on the morning of April 24th, in the early hours before dawn, they began pouring artillery fire on the positions of the 2nd Battalion. It was there that they chose to launch their counterattack. They wanted that hill because from it they could command the countryside with their fire. If that attack had succeeded the whole (U.S.) advance would have been seriously jeopardized.*
>
> *Later it was learned that the German artillery fire on the hill came from a fairly heavy concentration of pieces. There were two batteries of 88s (a little larger than our three-inch gun) and at least one battery of something heavier, probably 105s.*
>
> *Now the artillery fire lifted and Major Dilley could see the German batteries and he directed our own field artillery fire against them. Over on the other flank was a strong German point with heavy mortars dug into the rock hillside, and these mortars too were firing on Nelson's battalion.*
>
> *The boys knew from this (the shelling) that the counterattack was coming and presently they could see the Germans coming at them, a man here, a man there, small squads of advances from rock to rock.*
>
> *Now the artillery fire lifted and Major Dilley, looking up on*

Nelson's hill, could see little figures ducking from rock to rock, stopping to fire, throwing themselves on the ground and tossing grenades. It was too far for him to tell which were Americans and which Germans.

At this stage of a fight, formations cease to have meaning. The men fight in small groups, every man for himself, shooting or throwing a grenade when he sees an enemy. To a distant observer it doesn't mean much. To the man on the ground it is a grim game of hide-and-seek, taut nerves and super-alert senses, with knowledge that the man who moved faster was the winner.

Nelson's mortars, Dilley said, undoubtedly were firing as a battery of six guns and Nelson himself was an observer for them. That meant that he had to go forward until he could see the enemy. He made his way through the brush and around rock until he came over the slope where he could see the Germans and direct fire on them. He probably used hand signals to direct the fire of his guns.

As he was doing this German artillery fire resumed, probably the Germans were trying to find and silence the very mortars that Nelson was directing. Meanwhile, advanced German infantrymen were shooting at him.

The fire of Nelson's battery must have been extremely effective. The Germans didn't like it. To the mortar fire goes much of the credit for stopping the counterattack and this testifies to its effectiveness.

Nelson was wounded by an explosion. The doctors I have talked to say that he probably didn't feel pain. Wounded men at Walter Reed (Army Hospital), seriously wounded, bear this out. About all a man feels is numbness, no sensation at all.

So Nelson, in spite of his wound, climbed higher up on the hill where he could see better. There were Germans only a few yards ahead of him. One of them probably threw a hand grenade.

Through all of this, in spite of his wounds, your husband was so intent upon his job that he continued to direct fire until he lost consciousness.

An eyewitness account of the disposition of Sergeant Nelson's remains was broadcast over Station WILM on its Memorial Day Program in 1948 by Sergeant Victor Kowalski, a fellow member of H Company and Wilmingtonian. Kowalski said in part:

After any battle you usually ask one another the question, 'Who did they get?' meaning who was killed? One of the names I heard was 'Bill Nelson' so I started in the direction where he was last seen. I found Sergeant Bill Nelson lying where he had fallen. He died like a real soldier, 'in action.'

Sergeant Westfall and I took Sergeant Nelson's body to the other side of the command post with all of the other dead that were killed in the past fight. After all the dead and wounded had been collected we started preparing for our descent from the mountains. We tied Sergeant Nelson's body across the saddle of one of the mules along with all of his dead comrades. Those wounded who could sit were put on the mules, and those severely wounded were put on litters and carried by German soldiers who were captured in the fight. Those wounded who could walk brought up the rear of the column.

The trip was a slow tortuous procession that lasted nearly seven hours. It was a sight which I never will forget. As we neared the bottom we passed new replacements going up to the front to take the places of those who were killed and wounded. When we arrived at the assembly area the chaplains of the three faiths were waiting for us. What an exchange, we take up food and water and bring back dead and wounded.

The chaplains wasted no time when the bodies were brought in. Sergeant Westfall and I laid Sergeant Nelson's body beside those of his dead comrades. The war was over for them. For Bill Nelson, he died a soldier's death and he was really missed by all of his buddies from his homestate, friends Carey, Shallcross, Parker and myself. The chaplains covered all the bodies with blankets and laid them side by side in an Army truck, and it was on its way to the divisional burial ground.

I watched the truck as it pulled away and rounded the bend. There was still a war to be fought so my buddy and I left the chaplains to prepare another load for the front.

Sergeant William L. Nelson of Delaware and H Company, 60th Infantry, later had a Liberty ship named for him. There is an armory with his name on it in his home town of Middletown and in Legislative Hall of the State Capitol in Dover hangs his portrait that was commissioned by fellow workers at Hercules Powder Company. A copy of that portrait hangs in a recreation center named for Nelson at Fort Lewis, Washington and a copy of the portrait and Nelson's citation for award of the Medal of Honor are to be found on the dedication page of this book.

The valiant defense of Djebel Dardyss by the 60th Infantry's 2nd Battalion attracted much attention from generals and news reporters. In the weeks ahead Major Mike Kauffman worked diligently to get his unit's accomplishment recognized for he realized the value of this in building morale and cohesiveness for the even tougher battles that lay ahead.

2nd Lieutenant Irving Sussman,[10] Major Kauffman's intelligence officer at Djebel Dardyss, recalls of his commander:

> *Mike Kauffman is a hyperactive, tireless romantic, a dreamer, as poorly designed to be a soldier, perhaps, as the corporate executive he later became in life. He's the man who took a crazy New York kid named 'Mollie' and made him his trusted orderly and chauffeur. It didn't make sense but it worked. Mike is the heroic-type, the point man of a bunch of us advancing single file through the brush when the German soldiers were so near we could hear them chattering. Then, with hand signals, he'd get us deployed and firing our M1s to do the job.*
>
> *Moving on to Djebel Dardyss silently, under cover of fading light, we spread out and dug in with a strange hushed silence with barely enough light to make out the fellow working on the next hole. I remember thinking how it was like being led into a dark theater after the movie had started. Lieutenants and privates alike, we were all crammed together as in an audience.*
>
> *Suddenly, the slow music was done. The skies were being lit up by shelling. The pounding was unbelievable and seemed to be endless. We had received replacements fresh from the States shortly before starting this attack. Now I found myself staring into the face of this Chinese kid who had been among them, now down on all fours just a few feet away, Strangely, I wanted to laugh for he seemed to be imploring me to make the terror stop. It was so crazy and I felt such a pity for this kid, so frightened but not uttering a sound. In a flash of light I could see that he had only managed to scrape a few inches from his hole.*
>
> *We stayed on Djebel Dardyss through the shelling and then the counterattack because Mike was there and our leader wanted us to stay with him. He was always the leader, the boss, the guy we all followed.*

1st Lieutenant Douglas M. Gover was assistant surgeon of the 2nd Battalion:

> *The Battalion moved onto Djebel Dardyss late in the afternoon. The Germans counterattacked through the following morning. Our men started to retreat but they were rallied by their leaders. Then, with the superior firepower of their M1s for the most part, they prevailed. The Germans fell back and withdrew.*
>
> *Our aid station, such as it was, was situated in the open on*

the west side of the hill. The wounded were treated there then hand-carried by stretcher down the mountain. The Germans left a lot of equipment and grenades behind and I remember avoiding them for fear that they were booby-trapped. We followed the Germans for the next few days and there were skirmishes with Italian sailors that the Germans left behind to cover their retreat. They would harass us with mortar fire, then our artillery observers would zero-in some of our stuff and that would take care of it rather quickly.

Our movements were all cross-country and a trail was being constructed behind us as we advanced. We never stayed still long enough to put up a proper aid station. Our commander, Mike Kauffman was something of a character but a fine officer. He inspired his men and they had confidence in him. I served under seven different battalion commanders during the war and Mike was the most outstanding.

The 60th's 2nd Battalion broke the back of German resistance in the sector north of the Sedjenane river. Never again did the Germans attempt to hold a line or maneuver against the advancing Americans here. This signal victory was immediately recognized as such and the battalion became the first infantry unit of the 9th Division to be awarded the Distinguished Unit Citation, which concluded:

The gallant and intrepid conduct of this entire battalion afforded a great tactical advantage in seizing and holding dominating terrain and assisted the advance of our forces culminating in the defeat of German arms in North Africa.

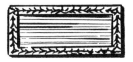

The 60th Infantry paused for a day to reorganize and then continued its advance, hop-scotching on to its successive objectives, carefully securing each in turn before continuing. By April 26th it was outpacing the CFA to the north and its direction of advance was shifted to the northeast in order to help the French attain their objectives. On the 28th the 60th secured Kef Sahan, a feature 2.3 miles northeast of Djebel M'rata.

The adjustment of sectors facilitated the CFA's closing on their opposition. On 30 April it moved forward to Djebel Tauro and captured over 200 prisoners, mostly Italians. The next day it gathered up over 500 more.[11] This effectively smashed the right wing of the Division von Manteuffel. The CFA moved next to the southeast towards Djebel Cheniti.

Intelligence reports by this time were confirming suspicions that the Germans would rally on Kef en Nsour, a dominant feature assigned to the CFA, as well as on Djebel Cheniti, the last key defensive positions before reaching the coastal plain. Accordingly, it was decided to switch responsibility for taking Kef en Nsour to the 3rd Battalion, 60th Infantry. However, by this time, logistic factors of time and space had replaced the enemy as the main obstacle to progress. The troops were simply not getting enough to eat to maintain their original pace.

Technical Sergeant Charles S. Willsher, 3rd Battalion, recorded in his journal:[12]

> *Then we started a 17-mile hike through the mountains toward the port of Bizerte on the Mediterranean. It was really tough going with no roads. We were being supplied by mules which had further to go each day because we kept pushing forward. The guys who were fighting with those stubborn mules were from our kitchen and pioneer sections and they really had their hands full. It was almost a 24-hour-a-day job and the further we went, the worse it got. Mules were being used up and the men were in as rough shape. No rest and there were days when the GIs had to share one can of C-rations and very little water.*

Added to these woes for General Eddy was growing pressure from higher headquarters to speed up the advance in order to beat the British into Bizerte. There were also additional problems with leadership of the Go Devils.

Early on in the operation it had become necessary to get rid of the 60th's executive officer, Colonel Joseph A. Teece, ostensibly because he held a rank higher than that authorized for his job. Actually Teece had been promoted five months earlier and it did not seem to concern anyone until someone, perhaps Teece himself or possibly one of the 60th's battalion commanders, asserted to General Eddy that most of the regiment's officers preferred Teece's leadership to that of deRohan. The commander, it was said, would not come forward to discuss problems or to provide encouragement. Faced with this charge, which was apparently a complete surprise to Eddy, it was thought imperative to get rid of Teece.[13]

On the heels of this event, Colonel deRohan became ill on the morning of April 30th and had to be evacuated. Lt. Colonel Conway, who had been waiting for an assignment to the 9th, was sent down as executive officer and acting regimental commander. Colonel George

B. Barth, the 9th's chief of staff, recorded:[14]

> *Colonel deRohan had commanded the 60th at the Port Lyautey landing and later at Maknassy where the regiment, attached to the 1st Armored Division, had a long, frustrating experience similar to that of the rest of the 9th Division at El Guettar. He was over 50 years old and probably should not have been subjected to the physical rigors of regimental command. (The War Department policy at that time was that regimental commanders should be under age 45 when assigned). In Northern Tunisia Colonel deRohan was taken sick. We needed a good colonel and we needed him at once. Our need was met from an unexpected source. Lt. Colonel Theodore J. Conway, a young American from the staff of 18th Army Group, was assigned directly to the 9th Infantry Division and was given command of the 60th Infantry which was making the main effort of the Division on our northern flank.*
>
> *General Eddy was not in the CP so I briefed Colonel Conway before sending him forward. I told him that the objectives of the 60th Infantry were (1) capture of Kef Nsour (Hill 423), (2) capture of Hill 499 north of the Sedjenane-Bizerte road, and (3) capture by assault of the heights of Djebel Cheniti (Hill 209). Objective 3 was to take place three days after the capture of Objectives 1 and 2 by the 60th Infantry. I would see him later that morning.*
>
> *When I reached the old 60th Infantry CP it was closed. An MP said it was somewhere to the east along the main supply road. I found Conway at his new command post about seven miles east of the old CP. It was near the CP of his leading battalion. He was busy preparing plans for the employment of the regiment against Objectives 1 and 2. My spirits rose immediately because I knew that we had been given a young, vigorous leader who could be depended on to take over our main attack and push it to the limit.*

Again in his journal Technical Sergeant Charles S. Willsher of the 3rd Battalion described the advent of a new regimental commander on May 2nd:[15]

> *The regimental executive officer (Lt. Col. Conway) arrived at the Battalion CP at 1000 (and) pointed out that an error had been made in (reporting) the location of the Battalion CP. (Conway) ordered the Battalion CO (Major Dilley) to attack and capture the Division objective. (Dilley) issued orders for Company K to attack hill at J440895. The Company K, with elements of M,*

*attack went very well and the rest of the Battalion along with
Company K marched to the Division objective.*

Major Rudolf Witzig, 11th Parachute Engineer Battalion,
recorded:[16]

*Until May 1st we retreated step by step. We are now
'Kampfgruppe Witzig' consisting of what is left of my unit, remnants of the Deutsch-Arabische Lehr Abteilung, and an attached
rehabilitation company which we called the 'Black Market
Butchers' (remnants of the 962nd Afrika Schuetzen Regiment).
Our last line runs from the Fiddadam Hills to Kef en Nsour,
about ten kilometers north of the Jefna Pass.*

*On May 1st the Americans definitely break through in an
easterly direction towards Bizerte. The (Manteuffel) Division
retreats toward the southeast and abandons Mateur. The battalion is relieved and used as a construction company.*

General Lothar Bro'sch-Foraheim, now retired from the Aus-
trian Army but then commanding the 1st Schwachran, Schnellabteil-
ung 334, remembers that late in April 1943, following severe fighting
west of Kairouan, what remained of the battalion was consolidated in
his unit to be attached to the Division Manteuffel in Northern Tunisia.
He reported to General von Manteuffel in Mateur and was assigned to
Major Witzig's command to reinforce defenses extending southwest
from Kef en Nsour. Lieutenant Bro'sch-Fohraheim then commanded
about 120 men. Witzig did not have many more. Together these
forces could do little more than spread out on the high ground in a
series of strongpoints with a few heavy machineguns and mortars.

General von Manteuffel told the young officer:

*I anticipate in your sector only minor U.S. or French forces
and you surely will be able to hold them. I don't believe the
Americans will want to attack in this extremely difficult terrain
so I assume that the enemy reasonably will put his main effort in
a thrust out of the Sedjenane valley and there we must hold as
long as possible. If the Americans get out of the Sedjenane it will
be a matter of days before the Allies are in Tunis, the capital.*

In the new positions after a few days without contact except for
harassing U.S. artillery fire, Major Witzig suggested to the lieutenant
that each force provide a platoon to make a coordinated attack on an
American artillery OP located in front of their positions.
Bro'sch-Foraheim was opposed since he thought the position might be
strongly held but Witzig insisted. At midnight the officers heard heavy

infantry firing in the OP's direction and then it became quiet. That was the last seen or heard of the attackers. Soon thereafter Bro'sch-Foraheim was told to move his force to Djebel Ichkeul before daylight and a few days later he was finally ordered to surrender at that prominent location.

1st Lieutenant Harold W. Smith, commanding L Company, remembers of this time:

> *On Easter Sunday, April 25th, I was under some scrub trees in the middle of a sloping open field. We were under long-range artillery fire but it was only close enough to make us keep our heads down. The ground was too rocky to dig in. I saw a man crawling towards us and, at about ten feet distance and from a prone position, he saluted. It was the only time during the war that I was saluted belly-down. 2nd Lieutenant Marshall Potter was a new officer and most welcome.*
>
> *A few days later we were preparing an attack and Potter's platoon was to take the lead. 'But sir,' he said, 'I've never led an attack before.' I answered that there was a first time for everything. Potter did just fine.*
>
> *The 60th Field Artillery with its 105mm howitzers was splendid. On one occasion, however, when my battalion commander had asked me to direct some fire, I asked for a 'ladder of fire,' meaning that several rounds should be fired in the same direction but with increased range for each shot. It would give me a line on the gun positions. But the artillery refused since it would give the same information to the enemy. I then requested a smoke round. Over the phone I heard, 'On the way!' and shortly there was a hell of an explosion and smoke billowing up only 50 yards away. I asked what that was and the artilleryman calmly answered that they always sent a round of high explosive along with requests for smoke, 'just in case we're on target.'*

1st Lieutenant Louis M. Prince, 60th Field Artillery, jotted in his notebook:

> <u>*Tuesday, April 27th, 1943.*</u> *Last night we made the most difficult move I've ever seen made in the Army. No moon, fog and rain made it so pitch black that we had to lead the vehicles on foot most of the way over the mountainous cross-country Arab trails. It took us six hours to go seven and a half miles. Two trucks broke down in our battery. That we ever got here is a miracle.*
>
> *As all of the other officers are manning OPs, it makes back-breaking work for me when we move. I have to go on reconnais-*

*sance, lead the battery and do all the odd jobs that we usually
have four other officers to do, besides handling the firing battery,
which is a two-man job in itself in this country and with the
amount of firing we do all day and all night. I think I've aged ten
years in the last week. I'm ready to come home. I don't like the
responsibility for the lives of all these men, picking positions
where we are defiladed and won't be shelled, etc., and keeping
from getting lost when we move. In addition, the earth is so hard
and rocky to dig in here that it takes hours to get a personal pit
dug.*

*Our last position in the mountains was the most ghastly and
difficult position to fire from that I've ever seen. Astraddle a tiny
mountain road, with guns on steep banks on either side. They
kept slipping down every time we fired and I could hardly keep
the sheaf parallel. We ought to have horse-pack artillery. The
ammunition situation was also critical during the whole time
which was another worry. I hope we stay in this position at least
tonight. We are all so terribly tired. Another move like this would
be awful.*

*Have seen lots of German prisoners. There aren't many Ital-
ians any more. The French 'ear cutter' regiment is still with us.
They seem to be pretty good. I wonder (with my fingers crossed)
what has happened to the Luftwaffe? I haven't seen an enemy
plane in several days and they used to come over in droves.*

*We are about 12 miles east of Sedjenane now but our objec-
tive, some Arab village west of Mateur, is still in the distance.
The 60th Infantry is suffering a lot of casualties. We have been
lucky so far in this battle. Several casualties in Headquarters
Battery but none yet in B.*

*Saturday, May 1, 1943. The last few days were ghastly. Not
more than ten minutes after I wrote the last entry (April 27th),
two German 155mm guns began to register on us. One over and
one short in range. From then on they laid them right on us. One
landed so close to me that the concussion gave me a sort of shell
shock and I'm just getting back to normal now. They must have
had an OP that was looking down our throats. Even at the time I
thought that if Jerry had as much artillery as we do life would
certainly be unbearable. At Thala we were shelled a little bit but
nothing like this. I believe artillery fire is worse than bombing.*

*The damage done, though, was remarkably small. Two
trucks were blown to pieces but only one man was killed. It was
miraculous that they didn't set fire to the ammunition or gasoline.
They shelled us twice for about 30 minutes on Tuesday. Then*

Tuesday night we fired a good deal so, by our flashes, they got a better line on us and on Wednesday it was awful. They laid them in, on and off all day, with only short periods when we could get out of our holes.

I tried to get headquarters to let us move our positions Tuesday night but they said no. I finally got them to move us up here Wednesday night and, although we were almost on top of the infantry front lines at that time, we were beautifully defiladed and everyone felt much better. We haven't been shelled here yet.

In the meantime we seem to be doing farly well. Soon we expect to have the Germans in this area surrounded. Major Buchanan, who used to be our Battalion S3 and is now the assistant Division G3, stopped by this morning and said he didn't see how the Germans could hold out in Africa much longer than May 15th. Let's hope he's right.

We are taking large numbers of Germans prisoner. One was a Pole who had only been in Africa for 20 days. They are losing about half the men and supplies they try to fly over here. The French took a tremendous number of Italians prisoner yesterday to our north.

Three men stepped on a mine on the way back here from the OP the other night. One was killed. Captain Thurtle, who was with them, said that it was through the bravery of the doctor who went through the minefield to give aid that two lives were saved.

2nd Lieutenant Joseph L. Rappazini was a replacement officer assigned to the 3rd Platoon, K Company, which he found in the hills above the Sedjenane river late one afternoon:

The platoon had come to rest high up on a hillside under an overhanging crag. In the course of that evening we heard men speaking in German just above us. Fearing grenades, we hung on not daring to sleep for fear of snoring. By morning, when we finished climbing the hill, the Jerries were gone.

At about this time, 2nd Lieutenant Chester Braune, Jr., General Stroh's ADC, visited the Go Devils positions. He found that the 60th Field Artillery had resurrected the pack 75mm howitzers it had come ashore with in Morocco and brought them forward on mules:

From an OP with binoculars we could see a German company lining up for chow. Out of range, even of the pack 75s that had been brought up close, they needed only 100 yards more after setting the ammo out in the sun to cook-up added range.

Again, the experiences of Staff Sergeant Wilfred M. Thornton, M Company, are described in *The GI's War:*[17]

> *The movement was rapid and the pace grueling. The men were living on a half a C-ration a day and filling their canteens from mountain streams which they hoped were uncontaminated. The battalion (3rd, 60th) advanced steadily for the next few days with no opposition. On April 26th it captured high ground overlooking the Sedjenane river. Here the Germans began shelling again and caused casualties, including the death of Private Schroeder. On the 28th the American company (M) was badly shelled and lost its first sergeant and a number of other men. The next day the battalion moved up a hillside, climbing all night, hit the top and came under fire of snipers, again with heavy casualties. Two really tough days. Then the Germans retreated once again and the Americans followed. It seemed to be a pattern which lasted until May 9th when the fighting stopped. The Americans came down out of the mountains, dirty, tired, unshaven with three week's growth of beard. Sergeant Thornton had lost 20 pounds and his buddies said he looked like an old man. Well, so did they.*

Notes

1. The 962nd Afrika Schuetzen Regiment originally consisted of courtmartialed soldiers to whom combat had been authorized for purposes of rehabilitation. The officers and NCOs, however, were handpicked from available Army rolls. At this time the regiment mustered only its own 2nd Battalion; other battalion-size elements of the regiment were the Deutsch-Arabische Lehr Abteilung and remnants of various Italian units formed as a battalion.

The Deutsch-Arabische Lehr Abteilung was another extraordinary unit. Cadred in Germany by officers and NCOs who had lived in the Middle East and Africa and spoke Arabic, the unit was intended to facilitate juncture of German forces from southern Russia and Egypt in Iran. They were thrown into Tunisia where fillers were recruited and training begun. The Tunisian Arabs were a disappointment. Most had disappeared when the cadre was committed to the frontline battle early in 1943.

2. Rudolf Witzig, *Das Korps Fallschirm Pionier Bataillon und I./Fallschirm Pionier Regiment 21, Januar 1942-Oktober 1944*, p. 12. (Oberst i. D. Witzig presently lives in Germany. This holder of the Knight's Cross of the Iron Cross is reknowned among the airborne for his unit's capture of the Belgian Fort Eban Emael in 1940. A copy of his unpublished manuscript is on file with the author.)

3. Ralton M. Speers, *History, lst Battalion, 60th Infantry, 1943*, p. 7. (The author is indebted to Mrs. Agnes M. Speers, 5 Patricia Ave., Albany, NY 12203, for the loan of her late husband's unpublished manuscript.)

4. Lt. Col. (Ret.) Matt Urban, *The Matt Urban Story*, pp. 191-192. (Published 1989 by The Matt Urban Story Inc., PO Box 2004, Holland MI 49422.)

5. James Lucas, *Panzer Army Africa*,(Presidio Press, Novato, CA, 1978), p. 184. Essentially the same quote is to be found in *The Tunisian Capaign*, by Charles Messenger (London, Ian Allan Ltd.,1982), p. 109.

6. Charles S. Willsher, *History-Third Battalion, 60th Infantry, Sedjenane Valley Campaign, 20 April-9 May, North Africa, 1943*, pp. 1-2. (Copy of this unfinished manuscript is filed by the author.)

7. Actually these were Italian soldiers who had been dragooned into German ranks from the streets of Bizerte. They had refused to fight and were under guard of German NCOs.

8. Michael B. Kauffman and others, *History of the 2nd Battalion, 60th Infantry*, pp. 20-22. (Copy of this unpublished manuscript on file with author.)

9. The author is grateful to the Office of Public Affairs, Delaware National Guard, for a copy of the Reck letter to Mrs. Nelson, and for the quotation from the 1948 interview of Sergeant Victor Kowalski on Station WILM found above. (Documents are on file with author.)

10. Lt. Sussman's surname was subsequently changed to Scott.

11. *Report of Operations, Headquarters II U.S. Corps, 15 May 1943* (National Archives, Washington DC), p. 9.

12. Charles S. Willsher, *Memories of World War II, 1988-1989.* (Copy of this unpublished manuscript is on file with author.)

13. From pp. 38-39 of the transcript of General Conway's post-retirement (1977) interview at the USA Military History Institute:

". . . In the 60th Infantry we had a situation where the regiment was divided right down the middle. Those who liked the regimental executive (Teece), who was a full colonel, (an) old soldier and in that group who disliked the commander, and then those who thought the Colonel (deRohan) was doing what he should. I can tell you. . .there were reasons for both points of view. However, what was totally inexcusable was that one group had written a petition and signed it and sent it to the division commander for the relief of the regimental commander." A copy of the transcript is on file with the author.

Research has not uncovered any petition or other reference to such. None of the former officers of the regiment contacted recall a petition or any discussion of the issue. It is possible that the officer who complained to General Eddy may have claimed that, if asked to state a preference, most officers would prefer Teece to deRohan. Beyond this, it is considered unlikely that any petition ever existed.

14. Barth, *The Octofoil Division Comes of Age*, p. 21.

15. Willsher, *History--3rd Battalion*, p. 6.

16. Witzig, *op.cit.*, p. 12.

17. Edgar Hoyt, *The GI's War; The Story of American Soldiers in Europe in World War II*, p. 191.

TAKING BIZERTE

By May lst the II U.S. Corps was moving steadily ahead in the north but the First British Army offensive was having trouble. General Alexander chose to reinforce the latter with armor taken from the Eighth Army and, while the re-shuffle was going on, Bradley was asked to mark time. The pause provided a point for II Corps' historians to end "Phase I" of its operation of opening the door in Northern Tunisia, and start "Phase II," exploitation to seize Bizerte.[1]

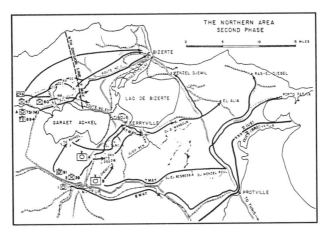

Map 8. Northern area, second phase.
(From To Bizerte with II Corps.*)*

It was not quite as clean a demarcation as the titles suggest. Some hill-slogging remained. Part of this was accomplished, however, with such style, finesse and unaccustomed publicity, that the 9th Infantry Division became something of an overnight celebrity organization.[2] Two reinforced rifle companies, independently but almost simultaneously, carried the ball in these May 6th actions. These were the assaults of Hill 223 by F Company, 47th Infantry, Captain Otto W. Geyer commanding, and of Djebel Cheniti by C Company, 60th Infantry, led by Captain Quentin R. Hardage.

For some time prisoners had told their interrogators that their leaders were planning to make a stand on Djebel Cheniti and the lesser hills on its north flank. Cheniti sat astride Route 11 which, on hitting the coastal plain north of Mateur, turned northeast along the shore of the huge water body, Lake Ichkeul, towards Bizerte. This was the only road traversing the eight-mile rolling isthmus formed between the lake and the Mediterranean. The retreating Germans destroyed the bridge crossing the Doumiss river, which flows out of the hills and empties into the lake just west of Djebel Cheniti and, from positions behind the hill, their artillery denied any daytime engineering to restore the crossing site.

The 9th's enemy now were mostly make-believe infantrymen retreaded from German and Italian base units in Bizerte and marched to the front where they were told to dig, do or die. Exceptions were light and heavy anti-aircraft crews now assigned a ground role, plus what remained of those reconnaissance units which had been attached to the Manteuffel Division at the start of the battle.

After their victory over the Italians north of Kef en Nsour on May lst, the CFA closed on Djebel Cheniti but could not cope with the well dug-in defense found there. They tried coordinated assaults on May 4th and 5th but could not overcome the defender's high volume of machine gun fire. The lst Battalion, 60th Infantry (Major Percy deW. McCarley) relieved the CFA on the night of May 5-6 and prepared to attack the following morning. In the meantime the 47th Infantry had moved by motor from the Green-Bald Hills area to the north of Djebel Cheniti and launched an attack to the east hoping to cut off the Cheniti defenders. This attack of the 3rd Battalion (Captain Gordon H. Sympson) also bogged down with the appearance of isolated enemy tanks and armored cars.

Early on May 6th the 47th resumed its drive east now with the 2nd Battalion (Major James D. Johnston) inserted to the south of the 3rd against the successive Hills 208, 223 and 205. All available artillery fires were brought to bear in support of the 47th and by 1000 hours, General Eddy decided that the enemy had been distracted enough to warrant an all-out assault by the 60th on Djebel Cheniti itself. This attack was ordered for noon.

The 47th's reconstituted E Company had had its first time "at bat" with the 2nd Battalion's attack. The preparatory fires did most of the work and then its proud commander, lst Lieutenant William B. Larson, found himself on top of Hill 208 watching the defenders occupy fall-back positions on Hill 223, about 1,000 yards to the east. Major Johnston, the battalion commander, arrived and decided that Larson's company would establish a base of fire while F and G in column would assault Hill 223.

Captain Ray Inzer, commanding H Company, 47th Infantry, remembers of the moment:

> *I was walking with Major Johnston's command group along a partially wooded ridge when we came under fire from some German machine guns emplaced on a parallel ridge about 600 yards*

to our right. We scattered and took cover, but had no weapons handy that were capable of taking out the machine guns until Lieutenant Russo of the battalion's anti-tank platoon got a 37mm gun into positon. After a few well-placed rounds by the gun crew the machine guns were silenced and we continued toward the objective.

After the battle Larson wrote an account of the classic action which followed. It was later published in Fort Benning's the Infantry Journal and in part is reprinted here:[3]

When it became apparent that they (3rd Battalion, 47th) could not advance it was decided that the 2nd Battalion was to push on from Hill 208 and take Hill 223. Since my company had made the assault on 208 we were put in reserve but were to support by fire the attack of Companies F and G. The Battalion OP was next to my own OP on Hill 208 and I had an excellent opportunity to see the whole attack and hear the reports from the various platoons during the attack.

Looking east from Hill 208 the ground fell away abruptly to a small stream about two feet deep and four feet wide with heavy bushes and trees growing on either side of the stream. Then the ground rose again suddenly to Hill 223. The highest part of the hill was on the left and consisted of a rocky knob covered with boulders large enough to give cover to a man in an upright position. From this knob the ground fell away to the right in a saddle and then rose again to another knob not quite so high but flatter and longer. From the high knob on the left a nose extended towards Hill 208. Located almost on the point of this nose was one of the two distinguishing man-made features on the entire mountain. This was a white Arab hut with a stone wall around it. To the right of this nose, as we looked at it from Hill 208, was a deep cut or draw in the mountain which ended just below the saddle. About three-quarters of the way up this draw was the second distinguishing man-made feature. This was a large cactus patch about four hundred yards square.

In general, the mountain and its approaches afforded little or no concealment. But there were some boulders and here and there a few scattered, scrubby bushes. At about 0900 on the morning after our own assault on Hill 208, the battalion commander (Major Johnston) brought the commanders of F (Captain Otto W. Geyer) and G (1st Lieutenant Lewis E. Maness) to his OP, oriented them on the terrain and the enemy situation, and issued his attack orders. He decided to attack in a column of companies with Company F leading the attack. The attack was to jump off at 1400 hours which gave the company commanders plenty of time to make their reconnaissance and issue attack orders to their platoon leaders.

As usual we didn't know too much about the enemy situation but fortunately the day before we had spotted some of Jerry's installations, and from our earlier experience with his methods of defense we were able to figure out where he would be located in strength. To our right front on the southeast lay Djebel Cheniti. All day long we had been under long-range harassing fire from Jerry machine guns dug in on the north slopes of Djebel Cheniti. We had been able to pinpoint about four of these guns and (Major Johnston) decided to fire one platoon of heavy machine guns and two 37mm antitank guns at these definitely located enemy positions to cover Companies F and G as they went down the east face of Hill 208, and before they came under the protective mask of Hill 223. On the forward slope of Hill 223 itself we had spotted one Jerry machine gun with about three or four riflemen dug in right in front of the white Arab house.

As you can see, Jerry sometimes does make mistakes in siting his weapons. In this particular instance, when he had a broad expanse of mountain which had much natural cover in which to emplace his machine gun, he had chosen to dig in right by a readily distinguishable landmark, and it was a simple matter to refer artillery and mortar observers to his location.

Patrols going down to the stream bottom and up the draw to the cactus patch had not drawn enemy fire and hadn't located any enemy in that area. From our OP on the north flank of Hill 208 we could see through the saddle and at different times counted as many as twenty Germans behind the right knob of Hill 223. We therefore figured that he would have several machine guns dug in on the reverse slope of either knob and sited to cover the forward slope of the opposite knob. We also expected to find prepared positions on top of the knobs and an OP at each flank of his position. (Major Johnston) decided to support the attack on Hill 223 by firing his six 81mm mortars as a battery from Hill 208 and a platoon of machine guns with one section on either side of Hill 208. These guns were already in position and required no change. For this attack the battalion had the additional support of one battalion of armored 105's besides the normal support of a platoon of the cannon company and one battery of our regular combat team field artillery (84th Field Artillery Battalion).

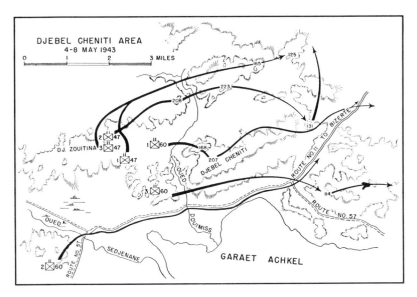

Map 9. Djebel Cheniti area.
(From To Bizerte with the II Corps.)

The company commander of F Company (Captain Geyer) sent back for his platoon leaders to be coming up while he made his reconnaissance and decided upon his plan of attack. When his platoon leaders had come forward (Geyer) first showed them the objective and the enemy situation. And then, since the OP was being subjected to artillery and long-range machine gun fire, he withdrew to a defiladed area where he made a small-scale model of the terrain using earth for his sand table. He then went over his plan in detail, using the model to demonstrate his intermediate objectives and different reference points. His plan was to send the 1st Platoon through the small saddlle on the right flank of 208 and have them work their way down a small draw to the stream bed. From there the platoon was to advance up the draw on Hill 223 to the cactus patch and then knock out the machine gun and riflemen located at the Arab house. Once the 1st Platoon had accomplished that mission they were to move forward up toward the saddle and up the slopes of each knob until they could bring fire on the machine guns believed to be dug in on the reverse slope behind each of the knobs. From positions on the knobs the 1st Platoon was to form the base of fire while the other two platoons enveloped the knobs from both flanks.

The weapons platoon was to go into position initially on 208 to support the 1st Platoon until it had knocked out the enemy machine gun nest by the Arab house. Then the machine guns and *mortars were to displace forward to positions on 223 where they could build up on the base of fire with the 1st Platoon.*

Meanwhile the 2nd Platoon was to move around the left flank of 208 and work their way down another draw to the stream. As soon as the 1st Platoon had built up the base of fire, the 2nd Platoon was to continue around the left slope of Hill 223 and come in on the enemy from the north. The 3rd Platoon was to follow the weapons platoon down into the stream bed and again, when the base of fire was established, they were to move around the right flank of the mountain and envelop the enemy from the south. If it became apparent that this plan wouldn't work, all platoons of Company F were to build up a firing line along the forward slope of 223 while Company G enveloped from the south.

Since it was impossible for all squad leaders to come forward and see the terrain, (Captain Geyer) directed that the next best thing be done--that each platoon leader make up a sand table model on the ground and go over the entire plan with each of his squads. The platoon leaders moved back to the OP for one more look at the ground and then rejoined their platoons to issue their orders and make last-minute preparations for the attack.

(Captain Geyer) decided to follow the last squad of the 1st Platoon, and although he had a 536 radio with him, he also put a sound-powered phone at the Battalion OP and had a lineman follow him with a roll of wire so that he could call back any urgent messages in the clear and have something to use if his 536 went out. This was standard procedure in most of our attacks.

At 1400 all the platoons were in position and the attack jumped off on schedule. The 1st Platoon leader had decided to send his squads down into the valley in a column of wedges with a five-minute interval between each squad. As the scouts of the 1st Squad moved off, the artillery started firing slowly at the known positions of the enemy machine gun by the Arab house and also on the places we suspected their OPs to be. The platoon of heavy machine guns on the right flank, and the 37s firing HE (high explosive ammunition) opened up on the Jerries on Cheniti. Meanwhile, the battalion on our right flank (1st of 60th Infantry) was moving forward frontally against Cheniti.

The mission of the 1st Squad (1st Plt., F Co.) was to work its way around the eastern edge of the cactus patch and set up a base of fire on the Jerry machine gun, while the 2nd Squad swung to the left under cover of the nose and assaulted the machine gun. The 3rd Squad was to take up firing positions on 223 to protect the exposed right flank of the platoon.

Each unit down to and including the squad thus had made its own provisions for establishing one part of the unit as a base of fire to cover the movement of the rest of the unit. The regiment provided the fire of the cannon company and attached field artillery to cover the movement of the battalion. The battalion commander provided the fire of the heavy machine guns, his mortars, his 37s and Company E to cover the movements of Companies F and G. The commander of F Company provided the fire of his weapons platoon to cover the movement of the 1st Platoon, and then the 1st and 4th Platoons were to provide a base of fire to cover the movements of his 2nd and 3rd Platoons. Despite all the supporting weapons thus provided him, the 1st Platoon leader made his own plans for fire support, making one squad a base of fire while the 2nd Squad moved. No matter how carefully the fires of the supporting weapons are plotted you must not depend on them. Provide for your own fire cover too. Even in the squad the riflemen did not move without first having the automatic rifle (BAR) down in firing position to cover their advance.

As the riflemen of the 1st Squad advanced from the stream bed up the draw to the cactus, the BAR team went into firing position to cover them. Up until this time the 1st Squad had not been fired upon, but as the riflemen emerged from the cactus patch the Jerries located by the white house began to snipe. The riflemen immediately returned the fire and in a few minutes the artillery began to smash volley after volley down on the white house.

Meanwhile the 2nd Squad had crossed the stream and was fanning out in a skirmish line just under the nose and worked upward to a point where they could assault the machine gun position. At that moment fate stepped in with a well-directed artillery shell which landed right in the machine gun dugout, blowing gun and gunner to Kingdom Come. As the 2nd Squad swept forward in their assault, the artillery fire, which had been landing barely a hundred yards in front of them, lifted. The remaining Jerry riflemen, seeing that their position was hopeless, tried to pull back through the saddle but were met by heavy fire from the 1st Squad and only one man succeeded in getting away.

The 1st Platoon leader now had a chance to look over the situation and consider his next move. So far he had made excellent progress. The first part of his mission had been concluded successfully with the able assistance of the artillery. As he looked to his right he could see that his 3rd Squad had now come abreast of his 1st and 2nd. By hand signals his squad leaders informed him that there were no casualties. It was time to put into execution the second part of his plan. The 1st Squad was to rush forward straight for the saddle. They would be covered by the 2nd and 3rd Squads who were now down in firing positions. When the 1st Squad got within 100 yards of the saddle, or when the enemy fired on them, the 1st Squad was to build a base of fire and cover the 2nd and 3rd Squads as they advanced up the knobs on either flank.

The 1st Squad moved out carefully in an extended wedge formation and were within 200 yards of the saddle when they received rifle fire from the top of the left knob. The BAR team, already down in position, returned the fire immediately while the riflemen hit the ground and crawled into firing positions. As the volume of fire from both the enemy and the 1st Squad increased, the 2nd and 3rd Squads in line of skirmishers began advancing up the face of each knob in a series of short rushes. Soon a machine gun behind the right knob opened up on the 2nd Squad and the platoon suffered its first casualty. Then the 3rd Squad also was fired upon, and now the whole platoon was returning the enemy fire. The sharp pop of the rifles and steady crackle of the BARs rose to a continuous roar as the 1st Platoon strove to gain fire superiority over the enemy.

The company commander had crawled up behind the 2nd Squad of the 1st Platoon and from his position was able to spot the machine gun and several Jerries behind the right knob. He immediately called back to the Battalion OP and asked for mortar fire. "You just fire over the ridge and I'll adjust from there," he told the 81mm observer. The mortars, however, were busily engaged with a more important target at the moment and could not give the fire called for.

When the 1st Platoon had reached the valley separating Hill 208 and 223, the 2nd Platoon started on its way around the left flank of 208. They, too, were using a column of squad wedges. The 1st had got about halfway down a small draw leading into the valley and the 2nd Squad had just reached the head of the draw when six Jerry self-propelled guns sneaked around the north flank of Hill 223 and started to fire rapidly on the 2nd Platoon. From his OP (Major Johnston) had spotted the enemy guns and immediately asked for artillery fire. The artillery observer called back the mission to his fire direction center and strangely enough was refused permission to fire. According to Division our tank destoyers were supposed to be operating in the area where the enemy self-propelled guns were and therefore permission could not be granted for artillery to fire in that particular zone. Since he could not see any of our tank destroyers, (Major Johnston) told the 81mm mortars to bring fire on the enemy guns.

In a very few moments the 81s were on the target and the Jerry guns started to take evasive action. They would fire a few rounds, then move a couple of hundred yards and fire again. However, the 2nd Platoon had become disorganized. Several men were hit when the first rounds landed. The 1st Squad tried to get down in the valley where they would be covered and the 2nd Squad tried to withdraw to the rear of 208. The platoon leader told his platoon sergeant to reorganize the platoon on the reverse slope of 208 while he went up to the OP to telephone the company commander what had happened.

It was just at the time when the 81s opened fire on the enemy vehicles that the company commander (with the 1st Platoon on 223) called for mortar fire (to support his 1st Platoon's attack). Rather than to wait for the 81s to finish with the Jerry self-propelled guns, he sent back for his 60mm mortars and light machine guns to come forward on the double. Within five minutes the 60s were set up by the Arab house and began to fire on the Jerries. The light machine guns went into action on the right flank of the platoon and swept the left knob with heavy fire. The artillery had started in again, smashing the Jerries on top of both knobs. (Captain Geyer) now had a firm base of fire established and was ready to start his double envelopment. Just at that moment the 2nd Platoon leader called on the phone and told (Geyer) what had happened to his platoon. After getting the details, (Geyer) told 2nd Platoon leader to bring what was left of his platoon over to the Arab house--and that he would use the 1st and 3rd Platoons to assault the hill.

Meanwhile the enemy self-propelled guns had withdrawn out of range far to the north and the 81s became available for fire on 223. From his vantage point (Captain Geyer) used his radio to adjust fire on the Jerries behind the right knob. Now the combination of fire from the 60s and 81s began to take effect. Jerries began to pop out from holes and behind rocks all over the reverse slope of the right knob and withdraw toward the left knob. They just couldn't stand our mortar fire. When (Geyer) saw the Germans begin to pull out he decided to act quickly and boldly. He sent messengers to the 1st and 3rd Platoon leaders telling them to assault the left and right knobs respectively--to follow an artillery barrage which he would have begin as soon as he got word that the 1st and 3rd Platoons were ready to move. The 1st Platoon leader, on getting this message, decided to move his 1st and 2nd Squads straight forward over the top of the left knob and move his 3rd Squad around the left flank to come in on the Jerries' rear. He had to send his runner over to the 3rd Squad with a written message but he was close enough to shout instructions to the 1st and 2nd Squad leaders. When the 3rd Squad had pulled back from the right knob and moved over past the Arab house, the 1st Platoon leader was ready to start his assault, and signalled the company commander that he was.

The 3rd Platoon had moved without incident behind the weapons platoon down in the valley where they lay quietly waiting for the 1st Platoon to build up its base of fire. When the 3rd Platoon leader received the message from (Captain Geyer) to assault the right knob, he decided to send his 1st Squad straight up the face of the knob while his 2nd Squad moved through the saddle and the 3rd Squad flanked from the south. In a very few minutes his squads were deployed and moving forward up the mountain. The 3rd Platoon leader signalled to the company commander.

(Captain Geyer) had told the situation to (Major Johnston) who in turn told the artillery observers. Everything was ready. Because the artillery was not needed at other points just at that time, (Johnston) had a total of six battalions of artillery to fire on 223. He didn't waste them. When (Captain Geyer) asked for his barrage, it came.

Both knobs of 223 suddenly burst into smoke and flames as the devastating fire of the artillery came down on them. It was beautifully timed and deadly accurate. As the infantry moved forward, the artillery fire moved too, always just about a hundred yards in front of the leading doughboys. The infantry in turn 'leaned into' the barrage and followed it right to the top of the knobs where it suddenly ceased while the 1st and 3rd Platoons swarmed over the top. They caught the Jerries stunned and flatfooted. The 1st Platoon striking at the center of the main German resistance charged with fixed bayonets and the Jerries broke and ran. The 1st and 2nd Squads immediately took up firing positions and started to pick off the fleeing Jerries like ducks in a gallery. The 3rd Squad had run into a Schmeisser pistolman hidden in a cave on the north slope of 223. The squad leader sent two riflemen forward to dispatch the German while he led the rest of the squad below the cave where there was a covered route. Then the 3rd Squad came in on the flank of the main body of

Jerries who now were running from the 1st and 2nd Squads. If the Jerries were frightened before, they were in a panic now. They streamed down the east slope of 223 into a large wheat field below and kept moving towards Bizerte.

The 3rd Platoon had even easier going than the 1st. Almost all of the Jerries had already pulled out from behind the right knob and it was merely a matter of walking in and taking over. Hill 223 had been taken.

While the platoons were reorganizing (Captain Geyer), who had come to the top of the right knob, called for and directed artillery at the Jerries fleeing in the wheat field below. The Jerries were hard hit and badly disorganized and this harassing artillery fire certainly prevented them from reforming for any immediate counterattack.

After checking with his platoon leaders, (Captain Geyer) found that the entire attack cost us two men killed and four wounded. The Jerries had left behind four badly wounded men and many uncounted dead on the east slope of the left knob and wheat field below. That night most of the company slept in Jerry-built holes, under Jerry blankets, and ate Jerry bread, butter, sardines and chocolate.

The assault of Djebel Cheniti commenced even before that on Hill 223 reached its climax. It has been recorded in the history of the 1st Battalion, 60th Infantry, written by Battalion Sergeant Major R. MacDonald Speers:[4]

Orders were received that the battalion would move out on the 6th of May to a position from which an attack could be made on Djebel Cheniti, upon orders of the Commanding General of the Division. During the remaining hours of daylight on the 5th of May, the Battalion Commander (Major Percy deW. McCarley) and company commanders made a ground reconnaissance of Hills 109 and 116. They observed from these points enemy activity on Djebel Cheniti and planned the best possible route of approach for the attack. The Division Commander (General Eddy) approved the route recommended.

Between the hours of 0330 and 0545 on the morning of the 6th of May the organization moved into an assembly area and awaited the attack order. At 1140 (Major McCarley) reported to the Assistant Division Commander (Brig. Gen. Stroh) at Division's advanced CP. The order for the attack was given at 1205 and, in turn, was given to the company commanders at 1225 for the execution of the prepared plan to take place at 1300.

Prior to 1300 a reconnaissance patrol consisting of one NCO and three enlisted men, equipped with a radio moved from the jump-off position downhill to the valley northeast of Hill 168. Their mission was to find out the enemy's dispositions and strength.

At 1300 C Company moved from the jump off position down-hill to a north-south line with the assault platoon in a line of squad columns, the other platoons in column of squad columns. Simultaneously, the heavy weapons company, D Company, less one platoon of caliber .30 heavy machine guns, and one section of the 81mm mortars, moved into position to support the attack. The platoon of heavy machine guns and section of 81mm mortars detached from (D Company) were attached to the assault company, C Company, so that they would be in position for immediate organization after seizure of the objective.

By 1330 the assault company had contacted the advance patrol which was at the limit of covered advance. D Company, less attachments, was in position ready to support the attack. No enemy had been observed on the objective up to this time.

Shortly after 1330 the radio patrol reported enemy 100 yards to its front on the northwest Hill 168. In accordance with the plans, at this time, a ten minute artillery barrage was placed on the area of Hill 168 by the 60th Field Artillery Battalion and the 62nd Field Artillery Battalion. This fire was directed from the Battalion OP and placed on the ground exactly as requested by (Major McCarley.) Under this barrage the assault company moved across the small stream of Oued Doumiss. The enemy opened fire with machine guns and small arms as the scouts reached the clearing before Hill 168, this fire being relatively ineffective. As the lead platoon advanced to within 75 yards of our artillery concentrations, this fact was reported to (Major McCarley) who then directed fire of the 60th Field Artillery Battalion to be lifted 50 yards and the fire of the 62nd Field Artillery Battalion to be concentrated on a small draw where groups of the enemy had been observed. At this time, the commander of the assault company, Captain Quentin R. Hardage, selected to commit his second platoon on the left of the leading platoon, the hour being 1415. The leading platoons again moved forward to within 50 yards of the artillery bursts which (Major McCarley) was able to clearly observe from his OP and thus directed the artillery fire successively up the hill as the men of the assault company approached the bursts. Soon the leading elements of (C Company) passed through and behind the forward enemy positions and were taking prisoners.

For the next hour there was (a) close-in infantry fire fight with the enemy fire definitely subsiding as more and more prisoners were taken. By 1510 all fire of the 60th Field Artillery Battalion was concentrated on the crest of Hill 168 and that of the 62nd Field Artillery Battalion was worked up and down the draw from which enemy mortars were commencing to fire on (C Company). Two enemy mortar sections were definitely located and knocked out of action.

By 1530 the leading elements of C Company reached the crest of Hill 168, and all artillery was lifted to the reverse, southeast, slope of the hill and to the saddle between Hill 168 and Hill 207. By 1605 C Company had Hill 168 under control and was quickly organized to hold the position while the support company, A Company, in an enveloping move, worked up to a position to the left, northeast, of (C Company.) During the organization of positions the enemy kept up intermittent small arms and mortar fire from positions on Hill 207. The support companies moved forward on the left of the battalion zone under concentrations of artillery fire, meeting little enemy fire and taking a few prisoners.

B Company, the reserve company, was moved through the positions of C Company to attack Hill 207 at about 1815. There were indications that the enemy was evacuating Hill 207, and a concentration of artillery was laid on the hill.

B Company occupied Hill 207 entirely by daylight on May 7th, having received only 10 rounds from several enemy tanks which were displacing along Route 11 to Bizerte. At 0600 the 3rd Battalion, 60th Infantry moved in from Hills 109 and 116 to the southern slopes of Hill 207. Friendly tank destroyer and reconnaissance units passed on the south along Route 11 moving east to Bizerte.

The Division Commander (General Eddy) personally witnessed parts of this operation and commended the group for their excellent coordination during the attack. This operation netted us some 40 German prisoners and furthered the advance on to Bizerte.

Colonel George B. Barth, the 9th's chief of staff, also watched the show at Djebel Cheniti:[5]

General Eddy and I witnessed the attack on Djebel Cheniti from an observation post on the front of the 60th Infantry. We had taken two days to perfect all plans and coordinate the efforts of the entire force. It was an awful but thrilling sight. First the artillery opened up with a roar, pounding the entire position from Hill 209 to the sea. The bulk of the fire was falling on the forward slope of the fortified hills. The concentration in front of Cheniti was very heavy. We could now make out through the smoke the assault battalion, the 1st of the 60th Infantry (Major McCarley.) Bayonets were fixed but the men were moving quietly. The enemy had "gone to ground" when our artillery had opened up and there was not a shot from the enemy position. Just as the advancing infantry, moving in deployed formation, came to a fordable stream at the base of Cheniti, our rolling barrage came in over their heads about 200 yards in front of the assault infantry. They forded the stream and closed in to 100 yards of the barrage. The barrage increased in range by 100 yards every four minutes, moving up to the crest of Djebel Cheniti. The infantry, moving at the high port and not firing a shot, kept their distance close to the bursting shells until close to the enemy trenches. Then the artillery barrage lifted to the reverse slope of the hill and the soldiers of the 60th rushed in, capturing or killing the enemy before they could set up their machine guns. Our casualties amounted, I believe, to four men wounded by artillery fragments while following the barrage up the hill. The 60th took a big bag of prisoners on the position. Only a few escaped towards Bizerte. When the enemy at Cheniti were overrun, the whole position north of Cheniti disintegrated into a rout to the east. It was a beautifully planned and executed attack.

Unfortunately, one error spoiled what may have been a total victory. After the surviving enemy had been chased off the hill, the victors stood about on the skyline congratulating themselves. It was not long before the sharp blasts of shellfire and cries for "Medics!" marked the unaltered capabilities of the German artillery.[6]

On Djebel Cheniti there were other casualties. Pfc. Joseph M. Foye, C Company, 60th Infantry, remembers that keeping a platoon leader was never easy:

A few days before taking Hill 168, during one of those 88 barrages, a fellow came running and fell into my hole. After a lull he introduced himself as Lieutenant Arnold Herfkins. I said I knew a Herfkins back in Hartington, Nebraska, who owned a grain elevator. He said it was his father. When I told him my name he said he'd watched me pitch baseball many times.

On May 6th, while out ahead on scout with Alex Hubbart, we got into a fire fight. I became separated and, after an exchange of grenades, ended up on a little knoll with seven prisoners. When the shooting stopped I herded them back to the CP where Sergeant Pinnegar told me Lieutenant Herfkins had been hit. He was dead when I found him--a bullet in the chest. His face was distorted and I couldn't identify him so I checked his dogtags to be sure. After the war I visited his parents.

I often think about the great training I received with the 9th Division. I got so accustomed to our artillery that I could follow it right up to the Germans' foxholes and be on top of them before they knew we were advancing.

Captain Alex T. Forrest, 15th Engineer Battalion, was at the Oued Doumiss to supervise restoration of the crossing site and he remembers of the moment:

One sight I will always remember was General Eddy being there to talk to the infantry going forward against Djebel Cheniti. I'm sure he thought it was going to be tougher than it turned out to be. The 47th's flanking attack to the north had been successful and this made it easier for the Germans to back off.

Our CO, Lt. Colonel Frederic A. Henney, was wounded by an S-mine during this period. He was an excellent commander.

Colonel de Rohan returned to duty and resumed command of the 60th Infantry on May 6th. With the taking of Hill 223 and Djebel Cheniti the end came fast for the 9th. On the left, however, the 47th's 3rd Battalion had a bit more fighting involving German armor.

Sergeant Joe Smith of M Company's lst Platoon was supporting L Company and he remembers:[7]

Sidney Schwartz, Joe Popeil and I were close together when a German tank came across a wheat field towards us, It was firing its cannon as it advanced. A fragment from a close one went through Popeil's helmet and he died instantly.

Captain James A. Garner, commanding L Company, 47th Infantry, recalls:

On May 6 we were approaching Hill 106 and stirred up a German Mark IV. It charged us, firing a couple of rounds, and then beat it. An M Company machine gunner with us was killed and Sergeant Adler of L was wounded. When we got on Hill 165 and I had a phone I reported to Captain Sympson, the Battalion CO. He said to withdraw but Colonel Randle, who was evesdropping on the line somehow, countermanded this order. It showed how closely he was following things.

It also brought support as 1st Lieutenant J. Edel Clark, now commanding the 47th's Antitank Company, remembers:

On the afternoon of May 6 the S3 called to have us check out a report of enemy tanks on our left flank. I saw no enemy but got a platoon in position to defend. While leading them my jeep went off the road and slid all the way to the bottom of the hill we were on. The first sergeant bailed out but the driver and I rode it down safely. Then the driver put it in 'grandma low' and we went right back up to the top. Soon after that a fellow in the halftrack in back of us accidentally fired a round from his Tommy gun. The .45 slug hit the fellow in the back seat of my jeep. Fortunately, he was wearing a steel pot which turned the round.

The only tanks we saw were 'friendlies' on Bizerte's outskirts where some of my troops found a cache of uncut rum, real thick stuff. We filled most of our water cans with it. We also liberated two motorcycles which Lieutenant Tom Laverty and I used that night to reconnoiter the waterfront. The moon was nearly full so we had enough light. The lovely waterfront homes were severely denuded. Walls had fallen away leaving the furnishings exposed like little girls' doll houses.

After our displacement to the vicinity of Lake Ichkeul the battalion and separate company commanders were assembled to get the good word from Colonel Randle. He was wearing his light-colored trenchcoat and possibly attracted an enemy observer. A round or two landed nearby. As usual he was quite unruffled and said, 'Let's spread out a bit so one round won't get us all. And keep your maps covered!'

2nd Lieutenant Roy K. Gordon, B Company, 47th Infantry, remembers:

Looking back on it all, one piece of advice I have for your next war is: Don't wear your best pants to the battle. I was shot through from one back pocket to the other. I called out to the newly assigned platoon medic, Private Pete Radiccio: 'I got an unauthorized orifice in the butt area and what are you going to do about it?' I was Pete's first casualty. As I recall his story: 'I took a shot of morphine for myself, and then one for him.' He then had to decide whether to be embarassed by the placement of my wound or perform his sworn duty to aid all nascent Purple Hearters. I told him to take the clean handkerchief from my right rear pocket and cover the wound. He looked around, mumbled a bit, and then said, 'Yeah, I found the handekerchief. It was in your left rear pocket. It probably won't wash out

though. You'll also need another pair of pants, or maybe a skirt.'
With that we let the war continue.

Pfc. Dewey Siddons of M Company's 2nd Platoon was supporting K Company of the 47th and he recalls:

*The platoon was moving out. All at once a German machine
gun opened up from our left flank. I could see smoke from the
gun and we went into action. I fired about 500 rounds into the
smoke and two Krauts ran out. Our lieutenant fired his lousy car-
bine at them. I really had to laugh. He was about 250 yards short
of target. We moved on and found the enemy's kitchen with the
sauerkraut still cooking.*

*Moving on we got fired on again by another machine gun but
finally made it to our objective and dug in. Then the tanks hit us
from front and rear with their machine guns. I could see a Tiger
tank about 800 yards out swinging its 88mm gun. Looking down
the length of that 88 is no fun when all you've got is a .30 caliber
water-cooled which could only scratch the Tiger's paint job. He
finally moved off.*

lst Lieutenant Ira Rosenfeld, M Company, 47th Infantry, recollects:[8]

*Our mortars did a terrific job supporting the battalion's
advance into Bizerte. Guns and ammunition were hand carried
and everyone in the company, including the officers, was engaged
bringing ammo forward. Accurate fire was vital so as not to
waste this effort, or to run short of support in a crisis.*

*At one point the attack was held up by German 88mm anti-
aircraft guns firing as artillery. When the mortars swung into
action, the third round hit the German's fire direction center. The
battery was completely out of action soon after that.*

Again, lst Lieutenant Lewis E. Maness, commanding G Company, 47th Infantry:

*We continued to advance toward the airport outside Bizerte.
The Germans by now were routed. There was only sporadic
opposition and mopping up along the way. After a couple of
days of this we came to a great jam of traffic and an armored
general officer, who was trying to straighten it out a la Patton,
yelled as we passed, 'Get those doughboys off the road and let
my killers through.'*

*One of my soldiers yelled back, 'Where were those killers
when we were back there in those hills at El Guettar!' The general did not reply.*

We moved to a rather high ridge from which we could see the German planes taking off at the airfield. We had out-distanced our artillery and they were out of our own mortars' range. Sometime later we secured this facility and, after turning it over to some engineers, we got on our way to Bizerte. Led by G Company, the 2nd Battalion of the 47th Infantry was the first unit to enter the city. As we did so some 20mm fire came from German positions across the waterway that connects the sea with Lake Bizerte but this was quickly silenced and the war in Africa was finished.

2nd Lieutenant William H. Horan, a platoon leader of K Company, 47th Infantry remembers:[9]

Shells and bullets were flying until our 84th Field Artillery Battalion opened up with murderous fire. The enemy tanks pulled back and we were given the word to get moving. We kept on and soon hit Route 11 which led to Bizerte. By then it was getting dark. We were dead tired and it started to drizzle. Word went up and down the column that we were going to Bizerte that night. We had cut off the Germans that had been confronting the 60th Infantry at Djebel Cheniti.

The thought of taking Bizerte seemed to renew our supply of energy, but the moment we halted we fell asleep and tumbled to the ground. The pace was fast. The physical endurance of our men was running out. But we kept on going, helping each other as we stumbled along on a dark, rainy night to Bizerte.

Captain Dean T. Vanderhoef, Assistant G2, says of this time:

We were becoming well-trained. I remember spotting a shiny Zippo lighter at the side of the trail. Scads of infantry had passed it by. The booby trap lessons had sunk in.

Private Spencer W. Norwood, G Company, 47th Infantry, remembers of the battle's last days:

We were just about to the built-up area of Bizerte when we were ordered to halt. Some French troops were brought up in trucks and they advanced into the city. The next day we all wanted to go and look over the largest city we had ever taken. Colonel Randle decided he would take care of that so he marched the whole regiment from one end of Bizerte to the other. After seeing what a mess it was in, no one wanted to go back. We ended up northwest of the city, bivouaced near the sea. Then someone got the bright idea that the troops should go back and pick up equipment left on the battlefield. We were trucked out and then spread out over the fields. Some fellows got into mines and a number were blown up. That ended that. We returned to load up in the trucks. As we waited our turn a truck backed into a field and hit a mine. What a mess!

As he walked along Route 11 to Bizerte Sergeant Martin J. Gill of G Company, 47th Infantry, thought back over the experiences they had:

I remembered how self confident we had become (without egotism) as we learned to cope with physical and mental hardships; to protect ourselves and each other; to deal with, respect and care for casualties. We often wondered how many more hills there would be for us to climb, dig-in and then, eventually, descend only to face another. Would we ever get something to eat other than canned C-rations?

I also recalled the dread of night patrols, the fear of incoming mortars and artillery, as well as problems with those stubborn mules while trying to get supplies up narrow hillside tracks.

We were on the outskirts of Bizerte. Most of the enemy had fled. The city was in ruins. Our mortarmen and sharpshooters were in the process of exterminating the few enemy snipers who remained. It was a rather warm, spring-like evening with a light, soft rain falling.

Pfc. Wilton M. Taylor, of M Company, 47th Infantry, recalls:[10]

We just kept plodding along that road to Bizerte. I actually saw men go to sleep as they walked along in the rain. They would stumble from side to side on the road as if they were drunk. When we got into the city about midnight we just flopped in the street. It poured down rain. For a bit I could feel it running off my face but then I just lay there and slept on through it.

2nd Lieutenant Lawrence J. McLaughlin, A Company, 47th Infantry remembers of that night:

It was one of the most uncomfortable of my life. We were stopped in back of a hill when it started to rain. There was no shelter. We had no blankets. I laid on the hillside and the water coming on the hill ran under my body in rivelets. The next morning I was so ill with cramps that I could hardly move.

And again, lst Lieutenant Robert E. Hulslander of the 47th's I Company:

It rained buckets the night we entered Bizerete. Captain Tan-

*ner and I were under a moth-eaten Arab blanket and farting like
mad. It must have been the rations. Tanner observed that if we
could only learn to control these farts the Germans wouldn't
have a chance. There was nothing more deadly than ration gas.*

And once again, Staff Sergeant McCully, of L Company, 47th
Infantry:

*Enroute to Bizerte mules were used to bring resupply. Some
didn't make it. We went down to a half a can of C-ration per day.
We sure got hungry but, when Bizerte fell and our mess crew
caught up with us, they prepared a feast. But most of the food
had to be thrown away. I guess our stomachs had grown too
small to accept it.*

Technical Sergeant Charles S. Willsher of Headquarters, 3rd
Battalion, 60th recalls:

*At last we got to the coastal highway and the mess sergeant
and his men could bring up water, food and our bedrolls. From
someplace he had secured a few loaves of real bread and it was
divided up among the entire company. It was only a bite or two
but it was real good to eat with our C-rations.*

*We had stopped by a small stream running down the moun-
tain. Everyone got into the shallow water and shaved each others
heads to get rid of the lice. With fresh clothes from our bedrolls,
a meal and a bath--what more could be asked for?*

*That night we captured the Bizerte airport and laid our
bodies down in the tall grass to sleep. The next morning we all
awoke scratching. The sand fleas hadn't had a clean body to
chew on before and they really went to work on us. We went to
the airdrome, filled our helmets with German gas and washed
our clothes in it to get rid of the little monsters. Then we put the
clothing on over those raw flea bites and there was more than a
little cussing going on that morning.*

And Major Arden C. Brill, executive officer of the 2nd Battalion,
60th Infantry, reflects:

*An unsung hero of this period was the regiment's S3, Major
Charley Fort. He is to be credited during these anxious days with
being the stabilizer of the regimental staff and the coordinator of
the battalion's movements. He tidied up the loose ends and was
always there with good, solid tactical advice when it was wanted.*

While the 47th and 60th Infantry Regiments were headed for
Bizerte, the 39th Infantry was attached to the lst Armored Division

and operated south of Lake Ishkeul and Lake Bizerte.
Pfc. George H. Seifert of the 39th's G Company remembers:

> *As we were moving towards Ferryville somebody spotted a German tank and sent four of us ahead to check it out. The Krauts must have laughed to see us do that as they had already zeroed in. When we drew near they started firing and we were hit. The next thing I remember was waking up in the hospital. When I rejoined the Company in July, I was told that the other three fellows were killed.*
>
> *So I don't recall our time with the armor as being a 'piece of cake.' It seems as though we spent all our time walking or getting shelled--not too pleasant when you are cold, hungry and tired.*

lst Sergeant John F. Lutz of Headquarters Company, 2nd Battalion, 39th Infantry, kept a journal in which he described the capture of Ferryville while the 39th was attached to the lst Armored Division:[11]

> *(On May 7th) we made the attack on Ferryville catching the enemy off guard and capturing many prisoners and valuable equipment, and inflicted great casualties upon them. During the time we entered Ferryville, the French people cheered and threw flowers at us, and gave the soldiers a good drink of wine. It was a great day for them.*

1st Lieutenant Charles Scheffel of A Company, 39th Infantry, recollects:

> *On May 5th the battalion was in a reserve position without wheels or artillery. We were on the south side of Lake Ichkeul and attached to the lst Armored. Sitting on the edge of a slit trench with a nice warm sun shining there was no way that everyone wasn't bedazzled by the poppy fields about us. The plains of Mateur are very fertile, much like a good Oklahoma wheat field. There were poppies by the millions. Looking to the northeast I could see a carpet of solid red for at least 25 square miles.*
>
> *A few days later we were south of Bizerte on the road to Tunis. An American staff officer drove up from the rear and alerted us that a column of Germans was approaching from the south on their way to surrender. In a couple of hours here they came, led by a large German command car flying a large white flag. It was a sight I'll never forget. There must have been 50,000 of them, some walking, some riding in all sorts of vehicles. We were looking at the beaten pick of the German army, Rommel's famous Afrika Korps. Most were young, like us. Their conduct was completely subdued and dejected but I didn't see a single*

German falter on their march. Apparently all of the sick and wounded had been left behind.

Again, lst Lieutenant Jack A. Dunlap, B Company, 39th Infantry:

I remember the night before their capitulation the Krauts put on a huge fireworks display getting rid of everything they had left, mostly out to sea. The next day when we came down out of the hills, unshaven, bedraggled and tired, the Krauts were lined up on the roads with their hundreds of vehicles of every description. As we marched by they appeared freshly-showered and clean-shaven. We looked exactly like the later Mauldin cartoon: 'Fresh, spirited American troops, flushed with victory, etcetera.'

And again the irrepressible Assistant G2, Captain Vanderhoef:

I was with the Division G3, Colonel Sundin, when he passed the word on the radio to our tank destroyer unit that the road was open and they should take off down the road to Bizerte. I played the 'William Tell Overture' on my ocarina into the mike as an accompaniment to the order.

Sergeant William H. Nelson of H Company, 39th Infantry had been wounded at El Guettar. Along with many adventures in the hospital and while returning to the front via the replacement system, he recalls being a witness to the disintegration of the German Army as it passed into captivity on May 9th:

I remember that road between Mateur and Bizerte with the many destroyed vehicles of both sides having been pushed off to the sides so we could pass. There were thousands of Wehrmacht soldiers passing in trucks or on foot, headed for their cages. For many years I was haunted by the memory of one German soldier who had been caught in his vehicle which had been set afire. The boot on the left foot was on the ground intact like he had been killed just as he was getting out from behind the wheel. The rest of him had been incinerated in the blaze.

The actual "liberation" of Bizerte was accomplished by an armored task force from the 9th made up by the 894th Tank Destroyer Battalion (Lt. Colonel Charles P. Eastburn) with Company A, 75lst Tank Battalion, attached. Along for the ride was a forward observer party from the 47th's Cannon Company led by 2nd Lieutenant Orion C. Shockley. The force made its way to the harbor area amid fire from snipers and artillery fire from south of the canal that connected Lake Bizerte with the sea. Shockley's group made their way to the roof of a high structure remaining in the city's ruins and began to fire counterbattery. The armor withdrew to the airport outside of the city. For that day's duration and the next morning until the CFA reentered Bizerte the Cannon Company party and 2nd Lieutenant John P. Ryan, still holding forth on his clandestine mission at the French Navy headquarters, could claim to be Bizerte's liberators.

"Journey's End," B Co., 15th Engrs., recon party at Bizerte harbor. (Army Signal Corps photo.)

1st Lieutenant Louis M. Prince, 60th Field Artillery, entered in his notebook:

> <u>*Friday, May 7th, 1943:*</u> *We just received word that the British are in Tunis. Bizerte fell this afternoon; the "ear cutters" and the 9th Division's infantry are now in the city. We are still in position about 10 miles away and we fired our last rounds about noon at some German tanks which are now captured. These last few days have been unpleasant but not so difficult. We fired about 4,500 rounds in three days.*
>
> *The Germans only had two companies left to defend Bizerte against the whole 9th Division and the French Senegalese and 'ear cutter' regiments. Jerry also had a three-gun battery of 88s which gave us a little trouble until this morning. They fired on us on and off, day and night in this position (which) they must have either surveyed or else used sound and flash, because we were hidden from their OPs. No damage done. We had deep, roofed-over fox holes, and had time to dig in ammunition. Of course, we were well dispersed. No one even hurt although we fired ourselves on a very important mission while the shells were landing in our position. One shell landed ten yards from No. 2 gun and although the men were standing up, no one was hurt. The 88 is not a very effective artillery gun. Nothing like the 150s that got us in the Sedjenane valley. Normally, of course, we stop firing and get in our fox holes during counterbattery unless the mission is extraordinarily important. The Germans must have had their guns set up on the beach practically because they didn't stop firing until the very end. We've had our usual great amount of (supporting) artillery since coming out of the mountains. I hope we didn't damage Bizerte too much. I'm anxious to see it.*

There was a flurry of tactical excitement when someone at II Corps realized that what was left of Fifth Panzer Army was backing up from the southwest towards Bizerte and might recross the channel there which connected Lake Bizerte to the sea in order to make a final stand in the streets and buildings of the city. This possibility was forestalled by building a defensive force around Colonel Randle's 47th which took up positions on the north side of the channel. The surrender came soon after that.

Again, 1st Lieutenant Ray Inzer of the 47th's H Company:

> *The most rewarding moment came on May 8th when we reached the high ground west of Bizerte where we stood and looked down on the city. We had come from the depths of El Guettar to these heights overlooking Bizerte. We had met and*

defeated the vaunted Afrika Korps. There is no way I can describe adequately the feeling which accompanied that instant.

It was hard to get used to the quiet at night. It took a while to get off edge. There was plenty to do, swimming in the ocean or catch-up work like taking inventory and reordering lost or worn-out equipment and clothing, writing letters to relatives of the division's 108 killed in action and recommendation for awards. There was also some silly and tragic "keep 'em busy" work like risking uncleared German mines in order to salvage equipment and ammunition from the old battlefields. Captain Otto W. Geyer, commanding F Company, 47th Infantry, will never forget one such chilling incident:

> *After capturing Bizerte we bivouacked outside the city on the beach to rest and swim. But not for long. At a commanders' call Major Johnston explained that the rifle companies would return to the ground just fought over and police it for bodies and abandoned equipment. I protested vehemently but Johnston said that the order had been sent down by General Eddy.*
>
> *Each day for five days we did this work, which we thought was a perfect chore for the German prisoners of war whose cages we passed enroute to the job site.*
>
> *Finishing work on the last day about 30 men of our 1st Platoon were headed from the east side of Bald Hill down to the road where they were to be picked up in trucks for the ride back to camp. They were walking in a single file led by a soldier with a mine detector. One of the men stepped out of line and tripped a 'Bouncing Betty,' the anti-personnel mine which pops out of the ground about six feet and then explodes, spreading hundred of steel bearings at high velocity over a wide area. There were eight men killed and ten wounded. Later in the day I was called before General Eddy to tell about this disaster. I let him know what I thought about using the fighting men to do this kind of work. We never did it again.*

Back at those wide, open and poppy-strewn fields around Mateur about 275,000 of the enemy assembled behind barbed wire cages. A very few of those that the 9th had faced off against had managed to escape that fate. Generalmajor Hasso von Manteuffel had been relieved for sickness on May 6th and was evacuated to Europe. Major Rudolf Witzig and a few of his paratrooper-engineers managed to find space on a small craft that made it to Sicily.

It was a major victory. Complimentary wires and letters came to the 9th and circulated to the troops. Here are a couple:

From General H. R. Alexander, Commander of 18th Army Group to the soldiers of that command:

> *Today you stand as the conquerors and heros of the North African shores. The world acknowledges your victory. History will acclaim your deeds. British, French and American arms have swept from these lands the last of the German and Italian invaders.*
>
> *As your commander in the field, I add my admiration and gratitude to those of the United Nations for this great victory, which will go down in history as one of the most decisive battles of all times.*
>
> *You have captured a complete group of armies and their modern equipment: 150,000 prisoners, over 1,000 anti-tank and field guns, 250 German tanks, many serviceable aircraft, and a vast quantity of stores, rations, and equipment of all descriptions, including a very large number of serviceable motor vehicles.*
>
> *Our Air Forces, which have given throughout this struggle such magnificent support to our Armies, have shot down in combat since the 21st of April, no less than 235 enemy aircraft.*

And from Major General Omar N. Bradley:

> *During the recent operations which began on April 23rd and ended on May 9th, the work of the 9th Infantry Division has been most commendable. The Division was faced with a wide sector which was extremely rugged and largely covered with an almost inpenetrable growth of vegetation. In spite of the tremendous handicaps confronting the Division, it pushed ahead, overcoming every obstacle. Its efforts were rewarded by the capture of Bizerte. The Division is to be congratulated on its brilliant performance.*

Notes

1. *To Bizerte with the II Corps* (U.S. War Department, Washington, DC, 1943.) p. 8.

2. The successful assault of Hill 223 was undoubtedly a basis for the 2nd Battalion, 47th Infantry, being selected as the honor guard for the visit of King George VI of Great Britain to the U.S. forces in Africa which occurred at Oran, Algeria, on June 14th, 1943. Lt. Gen. Mark W. Clark, then commanding 5th U.S. Army, presented the 2nd's Major James D. Johnston to the King as "the commanding officer of the crack battalion of the crack regiment of the crack 9th Infantry Division."

3. William B. Larson, "Hill 223," *Infantry Journal* (Sept.1944), p. 23.

4. Speers, *History of lst Battalion, 60th Infantry,* pp. 8-10.

5. Barth, *The Octofoil Division Comes of Age,* pp. 24-25.

6. Howe, *Northwest Africa,* p. 672.

7. Henry G. Phillips, *Heavy Weapons,*, p. 61.

8. *Ibid.,* p. 62.

9. *Ibid.,* p. 59.

10. *Ibid.,* p. 61.

11. lst Sgt. Lutz was KIA in Normandy. The author's thanks to James R. Todd for providing a copy of Lutz' journal.

POW enclosures near Mateur. (Army Signal Corps photo.)

"But We Learned, Captain. Didn't We Ever?"

Unlike the conclusion of our fight at El Guettar, that at Bizerte was sparkling clear and dramatically bold. This was Victory, writ large. "We won!" was foremost in every mind. It was an exhilarating experience probably known before only by those few men who had won by a knock-out in the boxing ring.

Nearly everyone grew in Northern Tunisia. The environment alone was enough different from that down south so that becoming used to it, and learning how differently it affected the job at hand, was mind-expanding. For one thing, we learned that dense vegetation not only reduced the enemy's ability to see you coming, but it increased his ability to hear your approach as one could not silently wield a machete or drag a mule up a path. Ways had to be found to offset this noise problem. Covering it with artillery fire was one.

Infantry-artillery coordination was much improved by the assignment of liaison parties from supporting howitzer battalions to the infantry battalions, something undertaken on Division Artillery's initiative. In addition to having observers present to call for and adjust fire, now there was someone constantly at the infantry battalion CO's elbow to suggest ways to use supporting fires while attacking or defending. The liaison parties carried their own radios for communicating with the fire direction centers and sometimes this alternate means for control was a situation-saver.

But, the most notable tactical improvement in the short time since El Guettar was having artillery provide close-in support of rifleman while they assaulted enemy in their dug-in positions. As shown so well at Hill 223 and Djebel Cheniti, it restored faith in the bayonet as something other than a can opener. It demonstrated down to the lowest level that "leaning into" advancing artillery fire, while dangerous to a degree, saved casualties in the long run. It is noteworthy that here the lesson was not something picked up at high level and promulgated as training doctrine. Rather, it was of "grass roots" origin by a few infantry battalion commanders. This said, credit must be given "the brass" for recognizing a good thing when they saw it. General Eddy made a point to do so in his summary of the operation: [1]

> *The 9th Infantry Division had entered its first engagement with the enemy, the Battle of El Guettar, greatly handicapped in not having had time for sufficient reconnaissance and in not having all of the units of the Division under Division control. Going through this battle, however, they had learned lesson after lesson, learning them the hard way.*
>
> *At Sedjenane and all the way to Bizerte, they demonstrated*

conclusively that they could profit from their former mistakes and take full advantage of the lessons they had learned. This they did. Time after time they maneuvered the Germans out of strong positions. They continually seized points of observation held by the enemy and, having deprived him of this, continued to drive him back. <u>They followed artillery concentrations closely, with devastating results to the enemy.</u> The individual soldier had proved he was capable. Commanders of all echelons had proved the same. The 9th Division had definitely become a capable combat unit. (Underscoring added)

Somehow in the closing days of the North African fighting a widespread rumor came to be believed as gospel truth, not only in the 9th Division but throughout the combat divisions of II Corps. This was to the effect that when the fighting was over large numbers of men, or perhaps entire divisions, would be sent back to the U.S. to cadre other formations or otherwise pass on the knowledge of fighting the Germans that had been gained. It will be recalled that a variation of this found its way into the notebook of the young artillery officer cited here. The story seemed so logical. Perhaps it had its root in communications between the War Department and the field about getting back the word of lessons learned. A handful of officers, for example, General Irwin, Colonel Randle, Captain Sympson and others were sent home for this purpose among others, and a few others, like Major Dilley, left to fill routine classes at the Army's service schools. But nothing of the rumor's scope was ever contemplated and, when events showed it to be false, it was devastating to morale. The peculiar thing about the incident was the general failure of the high command to detect the rumor and squelch it before it had so many believers. General Bradley recalled the situation in his memoir, *A General's Life.*[2]

Another serious problem with our GIs had arisen immediately after our victory in Tunisia. An inexplicable rumor spread like wildfire that those divisions that had fought in Tunisia had 'done their share' and would be returned to the States. For them, 'the war was over.' New divisions would come over to take their place in future operations. When the men were told emphatically that this was not true, there was widespread rebellion.

Bradley goes on to cite problems with the 1st and 3rd Infantry Divisions and concludes:

In part, I was at fault. If I had thought to inform the Tunisian veterans that their war was not yet over, the rumors would never have started. I should have made arrangements for the divisions returning from the front to be bivouacked at seaside rest camps where they could blow off steam before resuming the training for Sicily.

The problem described by General Bradley was certainly one that impacted upon soldiers of the 9th but not to the degree he observed elsewhere. This speaks to the division's better morale, stronger discipline and the leadership for which its followers were grateful.

While it was obvious that through the experience of fighting the 10th Panzer Division in the desert and hills east of Gafsa the 9th had become a leaner, meaner fighting organization, at the same time it had to be recognized that up north the division fought a weaker foe in both numbers and quality. The German Division von Manteuffel was not entirely a "Paper Tiger" but it could hardly be compared with the earlier foe. In terms of unit cohesion and skill demonstrated by its individual soldiers, only the 11th Parachute Engineer Battalion was comparable to units of the 10th Panzer Division. However, Major Witzig's unit was so depleted that it cannot be said to have survived its brief encounter on April 24th with the 2nd Battalion, 60th Infantry.

Given its superiority in number and firepower then, the 9th's success in northern Tunisia was as predictable as General Eddy announced it would be in his pre-battle message to the troops. The surprise was that it took as long and cost as many casualties as it did to do the job.[3]

Ninth Division combat losses (killed, wounded and evacuated, and missing in action) totalled 577 in northern Tunisia in a 15-day period. (In addition, 220 were injured, 240 were treated as "exhausted" and 429 were sick; a large proportion of these casualties were returned to duty with their units.) There were 508 combat losses in ten days at El Guettar, so the daily loss rate was somewhat higher in the south. Still, if the Sedjenane battle had progressed more quickly, certainly losses there would have been reduced even further. How might Bizerte have been taken earlier?[4]

It seems apparent from the record that the 47th Infantry was slow in bringing its part of the plan to a conclusion. This was clearly Eddy's fault rather than Colonel Randle's. If Eddy was as nervous about an exposed right flank as he appeared to be to his superior, he would not have wanted to aggravate that condition by letting the Raiders move too quickly to the east.

On the other hand, it is possible that General Eddy deliberately risked loss of reputation as an aggressive commander in Bradley's eyes, in a bid for further reinforcement. Bradley asserted that he could not have plugged the gap on the 9th's right flank without weakening his offensive elsewhere along the front. He neglects, however, to mention that the 3rd Infantry Division, while not technically under his control at the time, was physically at hand in First British Army reserve. Bradley could have asked for a regiment from it and Eddy may have been shrewd enough to angle for that. Another combat engineer battalion, however, probably would have moved things along faster than another infantry regiment.

Brigadier General Frank L. Gunn, USA (Ret.) recalls General Eddy as the consummate "front-line commander":

> *He was a very courageous, 'unflappable' leader who often visited the battalions and companies on line. He motivated their commanders to strive harder, and was quick to recognize outstanding or poor performance. The general learned the lessons of El Guettar and did not repeat the failures noted there.*
>
> *I believe the happiest I ever saw General Eddy was the day my battalion, the 2nd of the 39th, captured the German ground and naval commanders in a cave overlooking Cherbourg, France. He would have given us the city if he could have.*

While appearing "courageous" and "unflappable" to his subordinants, Eddy maintained a reputation as a "nervous commander" even after he became a corps commander in Patton's Third Army. Charles Whiting in his book, "Patton's Last Battle," notes:

> *General Eddy was very nervous, very much inclined to be grasping and always worrying that some other Corps Commander is getting a better deal than he is.*

Whiting goes on to qualify this criticism, citing Patton again:

> *All of them (his corps commanders) would fight any time and any place with anything the Army Commander would give them.*[5]

Lt. Colonel Bert C. Waller, USA (Ret.), has written with insight about the leadership of Generals Eddy and Irwin, both separately and in tandem:[6]

> *Perhaps the most significant element in their leadership was the exceptional ability to secure loyalty from their people. Some call this charisma; others say it is just getting the job done through the people they selected. Their integrity was unblemished. Their gifts of charisma may have been more inborn than acquired. It seems that whenever there was a crisis, either General Eddy or Irwin was there, with a keen understanding of the human strength and weaknesses of those they were privileged to command.*

Brigadier General Donald A. Stroh was another lieutenant who responded to the Eddy touch, making the whole of the team more than the mere sum of its parts. Colonel Dean T. Vanderhoef, USA (Ret.), is among the many 9th alumni who have reflected upon the influence of these men on their own later careers:

> *General Stroh was a complete gentleman in the finest sense of the word. Add to this, strength of character and professional competence of the first degree. He was in my mind 'Mr. Fort Benning,' the desired product of The Infantry School. In our personal contacts he was pleasant and open to whatever I had to say. The feeling of the staff was that Eddy and Stroh made a superb combination since their different natures yielded a fine balance in command.*

The 9th's "Braintrust" in action. Left to right: Brig. Gen. Irwin, Brig. Gen. Stroh, Col. Barth and Maj. Gen. Eddy. (Signal Corps photo.)

Eddy's charisma lay partially in the manner he gave undivided attention to the person or group he was addressing. He riveted with his look, and made the person addressed or listened to feel more humble or important depending on what circumstances required. Yet, his eyes would always crinkle at the end, no matter how serious the preceding conversation, to indicate underlying good humor and faith. Looking through the 9th Division's history, *Eight Stars to Victory,* one finds photographs of the general addressing newly-naturalized citizen-soldiers in Sicily or troops in pre-invasion training in England. Whatever the occasion, Eddy's audience was absorbed. The man made sense. He was listened to.

Irving Scott, then Lieutenant Sussman of the 60th Infantry, recalls a session with General Eddy which he expected to lead to severe disciplinary action. Sussman's explanations broke down the general's original stern manner. The eyes crinkled and the lieutenant knew he was "home free."

Pfc. John B. Knight, M Company, 47th Infantry, recalls of General Eddy's compassion:

> *My buddy, 'Big John' Watson, got a call at Magenta to report to General Eddy at battalion headquarters. It seems that John's mother back in Texas had read of the 9th and its commander in the paper so she wrote General Eddy and asked him to look out for her boy. John returned to our pup tent quite shaken that with all the men in the division the general would give a damn about one rear rank private."*

The old adage, "no man is a hero to his valet," did not apply in the instance of Manton S. Eddy's former aide-de-camp, Colonel Jacob. L. Riley, Jr., USA (Ret.). Riley served the general for five years in the postwar years. While an aide is several steps above a valet, the principle probably applies to both positions. When Riley was asked to speak at the 1964 dedication of the Eddy Bridge over the Chattahoochee River at Fort Benning, Georgia, he remembered:

> *Always accessible to anyone, he was a warm, understanding, considerate man who coupled a fierce determination to get the job done with a tremendous facility for working with people. It was this indescribable 'human touch' that endeared him to all with whom he came in contact. General officer or private, corporation president or janitor, royalty or commoner--he had the same unchanging smile and courteous manner for everyone.*

Acquisition of combat intelligence, while improved, was still a weak spot during the Sedjenane operation. Patrolling was much expanded, especially in the 47th's sector where it factored in the plan to deceive the enemy. But too often this effort's direction was blind. Commanders were following what the map told them and not going after solid information of the enemy's strengths and locations. They were not always hanging on to the German's coattails when he retreated through the bush. Never an easy thing to do, here it required aggressive leadership at every level to keep pushing ahead even after seizing an unoccupied position.

The 9th took 446 Germans prisoner in the north, as compared with 48 at El Guettar, and most of these came in the course of the fighting and not as the result of the mass surrender which occured at the battle's conclusion. There seems to have been ample opportunity through prisoner interrogation to find out where the enemy was next headed. The Division G2's problem in this area centered on a lack of qualified interrogators. Those attached to the division for this purpose were so lacking in basic soldierly skills that they took more time to administer than they were able to give to their primary function. In time, Major Robert W. Robb was able to develop his own team of intelligence specialists and this would bear much good fruit in later campaigns.

General Eddy probably paid more attention to intelligence functions than did most of his contemporaries because of some extended work in this area in the early years of the expanding Army. It was from this duty that he was promoted to brigadier general and assigned to the 9th as assistant division commander in 1942. His intelligence experience may also have contributed to a markedly secretive manner. He did not easily confide in others nor did he record his reactions to events or personalities. There was no Eddy memoir after the war. Yet the man was not noticeably shy nor uncomfortable with strangers. In Normandy Ernie Pyle wrote perceptively of him: [7]

> *One of the favorite generals among the war correspondents was Major General Manton S. Eddy, commander of the 9th Infantry Division. We liked him because he was absolutely honest with us, because he was sort of old-shoe and easy to talk with, and because we thought he was a mighty good general. We had known him in Tunisia and Sicily, and then there in France.*
>
> *Like his big chief, Lieutenant General Omar Bradley, General Eddy looked more like a schoolteacher than a soldier. He was a big, tall man but he wore glasses and his eyes had a kind of a squint. Being a Midwesterner, he talked like one. He still claimed Chicago as home but he had been an Army officer for twenty-eight years. He was wounded in the last war. He was not glib, but he talked well and laughed easily. In spite of being a*

*professional soldier, he despised war and like any ordinary soul
was appalled by the waste and tragedy of it. He wanted to win it
and get home just as badly as anybody else.*

Eddy was raised in a middle class Chicago neighborhood. West-
brook Pegler, a contemporary and later the Washington news colum-
nist, wrote of their high school days when both were trying to find their
niches and giving school authorities and parents some trouble along
the way. Eddy ended up in a military prep school, The Shattuck
School in Faribault, Minnesota. There with uniforms, rigid schedules,
weapons and prescribed values he found himself. A top student and
cadet, upon graduation in 1913 he was tendered an appointment as a
2nd Lieutenant of Infantry. Three years later, with war on the hori-
zon, he accepted the commission. In France, as a member of the 39th
Infantry (then part of the 4th Infantry Division), he was wounded.
Recovered, he was given command of the division's machine gun battalion.

Between the wars Eddy attended service schools, served as a
member of the Infantry Board for three years and on the faculty of the
Command and General Staff College for five. He had ROTC duty and
several tours of duty with infantry units. If he acquired a friend in high
places, it is not a matter of record. Eddy appears to have earned his
star on merit alone.

In spite of his misgivings about General Eddy's cautious side,
Bradley rated him highest of all his division commanders in Tunisia.[8]
Then in Normandy, after the brilliant battle leading to the fall of
Cherbourg, Bradley nominated him for command of XII Corps and he
led it for the rest of the war with great distinction as part of Patton's
Third Army.

After the war General Eddy was appointed Chief of Information
on the Army Staff. Later he became Commandant of the Command
and General Staff College, an amazing accomplishment considering
his lack of higher level academic training. While at Fort Leavenworth
he showed that he had never forgotten where his considerable reputation took off. A "division in the attack" problem was created for the
students in which, after a given situation, they were asked to select an
appropriate organization for combat. When the time came to present
the "school solution" a new instructor stood behind the podium, the
commandant himself. Eddy explained that this problem was not
hypothetical as they had been led to believe, but it was actual history;
this was the 9th Infantry Division in northern Tunisia in 1943 and this
was what worked and why.

Not long after that the new Seventh Army Commander came to
inspect the European Command Intelligence Center in Oberursel,

Germany. When time came to say goodbye, Eddy's eyes ranged over the assembled staff and spotted an Octofoil insignia on the right shoulder of someone he had not met:

"I'm sorry, Captain. I don't recall the name."

"Phillips," I replied, "3rd Battalion, 47th."

"Of course. Don Clayman's outfit. Were you in Africa with them?"

"I was hit at El Guettar."

"Well, we weren't so great then; but we learned, Captain. Didn't we ever?"

Notes

1. *Report of Operation, 9th Infantry Division,* p. 24.

2. Omar N. Bradley and Clay Blair, *A General's Life,* p. 172.

3. Brigadgeneral i. D. Ulrich Boes, now living in retirement in Germany, was then the operations officer (Ia) of the Division Manteuffel. He opines:

> *The personnel and materiel superiority of the Americans was crushing. My division was opposed by the mass of the II U.S. Corps. Presumably, it was then American tactical doctrine that, in order to avoid major losses, an attack would be attempted only when that sort of superiority obtained. The Allied Command never seemed to see through the permanent inferiority of the few German units in Northern Tunisia. Otherwise, they would have taken Tunis by Christmas, 1942, or at least Bizerte.*

4. Don E. Burkel of 138 Bank St., Batavia, New York 14020, is a student of German military history who interviewed and corresponded extensively with General von Manteuffel in the post-war years. The general recounted to him that by the conclusion of his division's 26 February-15 March 1943 offensive, the desperate tactical situation of the Axis forces was apparent and debilitating to every man. The Allied blockade was totally effective. Provisions of all kinds were rationed stringently. But while it was clear that no further offensive

action was possible, there was no talk of surrender, only determination to fight to the last bullet.

Early on 3 May the personal fortunes of General von Manteuffel changed dramatically. While observing the fighting of his Regiment Barenthin against the lst U.S. Armored Division northeast of Mateur he collapsed from a chronic kidney infection. Two days later he was evacuated on the last Italian hospital ship to Sicily. Command of the division passed to Generalmajor Karl Buelowius who surrendered its remnants on 9 May.

While it involved troops outside the sector of the 9th Infantry Division, another anecdote related by Brigadgeneral Ulrich Boes, the Manteuffel Division's last operations officer, indicates the fighting spirit which generally persisted among German soldiers to the end:

> *General Buelowius and I were standing with the commander of our anti-aircraft artillery, Oberstleutnant Hannemann, on a small hill southwest of Mateur when we saw at a distance American tanks which appeared to be headed in our direction. The general ordered Hannemann to reconnoiter their movements and report back. After more than an hour Hannemann returned with blood on his face and without helmet. He reported: 'Oberstleutnant Hannemann, back from reconnaissance and American captivity.'*
>
> *In a jeep with his driver Hannemann had dashed ahead on the road towards Mateur but they were soon caught by some American soldiers outposting ahead of the tanks and forced to load in the Americans' half-track for a ride to their rear. All of this had taken place under the eyes of one of Hannemann's 88-mm gun crews which he had in position covering the road. When the crew realized what was happening to their commander they fired on the half-track causing casualties among the Americans. In the confusion the colonel and his driver got away.*

5. Charles Whiting, *Patton's Last Battle*, p. 56.

6. Bert C. Waller, *Commanders We Knew*," p. 8. (Self-published in 1992 by Lt. Col. (Ret.) Bert C. Waller, 12944 Camino Del Rey. Poway CA 92064.)

7. Ernie Pyle, *Brave Men*, p. 394.

8. Bradley, *A Soldier's Story*, pp. 100-101.

EPILOGUE

Under Manton S. Eddy's leadership the 9th Infantry Division fought in Sicily, then sailed to England to join the great force preparing to invade Normandy. After D-Day it captured Cherbourg and led in the break-out from the hedgerow country. At this point General Eddy went on to a higher command. Under other able commanders the division continued as the wheelhorse of the First U.S. Army, participating in the Battles of the Huertgen Forest, the Bulge and the Remagen Bridgehead. Finally, the 9th met the Russians at Torgau in Germany and its work in this war was done.

Since World War II the United States Army has contracted several times with the colors of the 9th Infantry Division being folded and cased. Then, with some new emergency the colors have been unpacked. Now more than dust and creases are shaken from the tassel of battle ribbons topping those colors. Out come the memories and stories of what went before, the stuff of which a reborn 9th Division is given substance, identity and morale, its history becoming its being.

Sedjenane

Death's swift flight, through the April rain,
Paused at a place called Sedjenane.
With a cold hand he marked his prey
And picked the ones who were to stay, forever
At a place called Sedjenane.

In a brief moment, they gave their all,
Life, and all it meant, beyond recall.
Never to be bothered by the rain, they sleep
At a place called Sedjenane.

Wooden crosses mark each hallowed grave
And above the sleeping ranks, red poppies wave.
The fight is over, there in peace, they'll ever remain
The ones we left behind us at a place called Sedjenane.

(Author's note: these lines were written by the late John D. Day of the 9th Military Police and E Company, 60th Infantry. Thanks to Mrs Audrey Weber, Quincy MA, and Samuel D. Robinson, Swampscott MA, for remembering.)

BIBLIOGRAPHY

Books

Bender, Roger James & Richard D. Law. *Uniforms, Organization and History of the Afrika Korps.* San Jose, CA: R. James Bender Publishing, 1973.

Bradley, Omar N. *A Soldier's Story.* New York, NY: Henry Holt, 1951.

Bradley, Omar N. & Clay Blair. *A General's Life.* New York, NY: Simon and Schuster, 1983.

Brownlow, David G. *Panzer Baron.* Quincy, MA: The Christopher Publishing House, 1975.

Collins, Joseph L. *Lightning Joe.* Baton Rouge, LA: Louisiana State University Press, 1979.

Coggins, Jack. *The Campaign for North Africa.* Garden City, NY: Doubleday & Co., 1948.

Eisenhower, Dwight D. *Crusade in Europe.* Garden City, NY: Doubleday & Co., 1948.

Farago, Ladislas. *Patton: Ordeal and Triumph.* New York, NY: Dell Publishing Co., 1963.

Howe, George F. *Northwest Africa: Seizing the Initiative in the West.* Washington, DC: Department of the Army, 1956.

Hoyt, Edwin. *The GI's War: The Story of American Soldiers in Europe in World War II.* New York, NY: McGraw-Hill, 1988.

Kreye, William M. *The Pawns of War.* New York, NY: Vantage Press, 1983.

Kurowski, Franz. *Der Afrika Feldzug.* Leoni am Starnbergersee, Germany: Druffel-Verlag, 1986.

Liebling, A. J. *Quest for Mollie and Other War Pieces.* New York, NY: Schocken Press, 1964.

Lucas, James. *Panzer Army Africa.* Novato, CA: Presidio Press, 1978.

Messenger, Charles. *The Tunisian Campaign.* London, England: Ian Allan Ltd., 1982.

Mittelman, Joseph B. *Eight Stars to Victory.* Washington, DC: The Ninth Division Association, 1948.

Phillips, Henry G. *Heavy Weapons.* Penn Valley, CA: H. G. Phillips, 1985.

Phillips, Henry G. *El Guettar: Crucible of Leadership.* Penn Valley, CA: H. G. Phillips, 1991.

Pyle, Ernie. *Here is Your War.* New York, NY: Henry Holt, 1943

Pyle, Ernie. *Brave Men.* New York, NY: Henry Holt, 1944.

Randle, Edwin H., *Safi Adventure.* Clearwater, FL: Eldnar Press, 1965.

Reck, Franklin M. *Beyond the Call of Duty.* New York, NY: Thomas Crowell Co., 1944.

Strawson, John. *The Battle for North Africa.* New York, NY: Scribner & Sons, 1969.

Urban, Matt. *The Matt Urban Story.* Holland, MI: The Urban Story Inc., 1976.

Waller, Bert C. *Commanders We Knew.* Poway, CA: B. C. Waller, 1992.

Westmoreland, William C. *A Soldier Reports.* New York, NY: Doubleday & Co., 1976.

Whiting, Charles. *Patton's Last Battle.* New York, NY: Jove Publications, 1990.

Reports

History of the 47th Infantry of the 9th Infantry Division, 1 January 1943 to 31 December 1943. Washington, DC: National Archives, 1993.

Medal of Honor Recipients, 1863-1978 (Nelson, William L.). Washington, DC: Senate Committee Print No. 3, first session of 96th Congress, 1979.

Report of Operation Conducted by 9th Infantry Division, Northern Tunisia, 11 April-8 May 1943. Washington, DC: National Archives, 1993.

Regimental History, 60th Infantry, 1943. Washington, DC: National Archives, 1993.

Regimental History, 39th Infantry, 1943. Washington, DC: National Archives, 1993.

Report of Operation, Headquarters II U.S. Corps, 15 May 1943. Washington, DC: National Archives, 1993.

To Bizerte with II Corps. Washington, DC: War Department, 1943.

Articles

Andrews, Peter. "A Place to Be Lousy In," *American Heritage* (Dec., 1991).

Henry, Thomas R. "The Avenging Ghosts of the 9th," *Saturday Evening Post* (6 July 1946).

Larson, William B., "Hill 223," *Infantry Journal* (Sept.1944.)

Westmoreland, William C. "Riding to Battle," *Army* (April 1993).

Manuscripts

Barth, G. B. *The Octofoil Division Comes of Age in World War II.* Unpublished manuscript.

Dickson, Benjamin A. *G2 Journal: Algiers to the Elbe.* Manuscript journal in West Point Library special collections.

Kauffman, Michael B., and others. *History of the 2nd Battalion, 60th Infantry.* Unpublished manuscript.

Speers, Ralton M. *History of 1st Battalion, 60th Infantry, 1943.* Unpublished manuscript in possession of Mrs. Agnes Speers, 5 Patricia Ave., Albany, NY, 12203.

Willsher, Charles S. *History--Third Battalion, 60th Infantry--Sedjenane Valley Campaign--20 April-9 May--North Africa-1943.* Unpublished manuscript.

Willsher, Charles S. *Memories of World War Two.* Unpublished manuscript.

Witzig, Rudolf. *Das Korps Fallschirm Pionier Batallion und I./Fallschirm Pionier Regiment 21, Januar 1942-Oktober 1944.* Unpublished manuscript.

(Except as noted above manuscripts are in possession of the author.)

About the Author

From the Infantry Officers Candidate School, 2nd Lieutenant Henry G. Phillips joined the 47th Infantry at Fort Bragg, North Carolina in August, 1942 and was assigned to M Company. He participated in the regiment's amphibious assault at Safi, Morocco a few months later and after that was wounded at El Guettar, Tunisia while leading a machine gun platoon. He subsequently served as company executive officer and commander, and a battalion staff officer, participating in the Sicilian, French and German campaigns of the 9th Infantry Division. He was wounded again in Belgium and Germany and was twice awarded the Silver Star Medal for gallantry in action.

Phillips was commissioned in the Regular U.S. Army following World War II, retiring in 1967 as a lieutenant colonel. His postwar decorations include the Legion of Merit and the Army Commendation Medal with Oak Leaf Cluster. In the course of his service he graduated from the Universities of Maryland (BS) and Illinois (MS) and the Army Command and General Staff College. After Army retirement he was employed on the faculty of PMC Colleges (Widener University) at Chester, Pennsylvania, and later moved to Lake Wildwood, California where for ten years he published and edited his community's newspaper. He is the author of *Heavy Weapons,* a chronology of the World War II adventures of his company, and *El Guettar: Crucible of Leadership,* an oral history of the 9th Division's first encounter with the German Army in North Africa.

Colonel Phillips is a Fellow of the Interuniversity Seminar on the Armed Forces and Society and a Distinguished Member of the 47th Infantry Regiment. He is married to the former Lenore Louella Lembke of Marysville, California, and the father of two grown daughters, Christine and Kathryn.

Biographical Index

Abben, M/Sgt. Fred A.: 12
Adams, Lt.Col. Clinton L.: 39
Adams, Capt. Daniel B.: 65
Adler, Sgt. (L/47): 129
Alexander, Gen. Harold R.L.G.
  (British Army): 49, 61, 115, 140
Anderson, 1st Lt. Burton W.: 67
Anderson, Capt. Conrad V.: 83, 89
Andrews, Peter (Amer. writer): 155
Angell, Sgt. Barney: 57
Barenthin, Oberst Walther
  (German Army): 39, 151
Barth, Col. George B.: 49, 51
  52, 61, 72, 74, 107, 114, 127, 141,
  146, 155
Beale, Capt. John P.: 82, 83, 84
Bender, Roger J. (Amer. writer):
  153
Blair, Clay (Amer. writer): 150, 153
Bleck, Cpl. Edward: 68
Blumenson, Martin (Amer. military
  historian): xi
Boes, Major Ulrich (German
  Army): 150, 151
Bond, Lt. Col. Van H.: 81, 86, 89
Bowen, 1st Lt. William C.: 37
Boyarkin, Maj. (Med60): 48
Boylan, Sgt. Joe: 100
Boyle, Pfc. Thomas J.: 86
Bradley, Maj.Gen. Omar N.: 1, 5,
  20, 47, 48, 49, 71, 72, 74, 86, 80,
  115, 140, 143, 144, 145, 148, 149,
  150, 151, 153
Braune, 1st Lt. Chester Jr.: 43, 81,
  111
Breitenberger, Dr. Ernst (Amer.
  physicist): xi
Brewer, Sgt. Burleigh: 44
Brill, Maj. Arden C.: xi, 134
Brooks, S/Sgt. Howard D.: 67
Bro'sch-Foraheim, Leutnant Lothar
  (German Army): 108, 109
Brown, Col. J. Trimble: 5, 7, 27,
  50, 60, 78, 81, 91, 84, 85
Brownley, Capt. C.P.: 20
Brownlow, David G. (Amer.
  writer): 153
Brugger, 2nd Lt. Raymond J.: 43, 44
Brusic, Sgt. Frank: 17, 67
Bryant, Lt. (26FA): 39
Buchanan, Maj. (G3/9): 111
Buelowius, Generalmaj. Karl
  (German Army): 151
Buffalo, 2nd Lt. Paul R.: 65, 66, 67
Burkel, Don E. (Amer. student of
  German military history): 6, 150
Butler, 1st Lt. William J.: 86, 91
Caban, Pfc. Stanley: 84
Campbell (B/39): 58

Carey, (H/60): 103
Carter, D.J. (I/47): 54
Carter, President Jimmy: 95
Cheatham, Lt.Col. Charles H.: 82,
  83
Chaffin, Maj. Wendell T.: 63, 68
Clark, 2nd Lt. Herbert E.: xi
Clark, 1st Lt. J. Edel: 65, 130
Clark, Maj.Gen. Mark W.: 61, 140
Clarke, 1st Lt. William W.: 36
Clayman, Lt. Col. Donald C.: 150
Clegg, Capt. Herbert W.: 55
Clouser, Pvt. John: 39
Cobb, Maj. Robert B.: xi, 76,
  77, 78, 87, 91
Coggins, Jack (Amer. writer): 153
Collins, Lt.Gen. Joseph L.: 153
Connolly, 2nd Lt. George I.: xi,
  19, 85, 90
Connolly, Pfc. Raymond: 56
Connor, Maj.Gen. Fox: 76
Connors, Chap. Edward T.: 57
Conway, Lt.Col. Theodore J.: 49,
  50, 61, 106, 107, 114
Corpening, Capt. Wayne A.: 45
Cox, Maj. Neil: 32
Craig, Lt. Cecil: 80
Custer, Lt. Col. George A.: 64
Dawson, Lt. Col. James T.: 39
Day, Pfc. John D.: 152
DeMella, Sgt. Nick: 32
DeNobrega, Madame (French
  nurse): 19
DeRohan, Col. Frederic: 5, 7, 50,
  97, 106, 107, 114
Derrien, Adm. Louis (French Navy):
  73
Dickson, Col. Benjamin A.: 155
Dilley, Maj. John H.: 97, 99, 101,
  102, 107, 143
DiRisio, S/Sgt. Albert: 85
Downs, 1st Lt. Stanford L.: 80, 83,
  90
Dunlap, 2nd Lt. Jack A.: xi, 12,
  57, 81, 87, 136
Eastburn, Lt.Col. Charles P.: 136
Eddy, Maj. Gen. Manton S.: 1, 2, 3,
  4, 5, 7, 15, 17, 26, 27, 42, 48,
  49, 51, 53, 60, 61, 70, 71, 72, 76,
  81, 106, 114, 116, 125, 127, 139,
  142, 144, 145, 146, 147, 148, 149,
  152
Eisenhower, Gen. Dwight D.: 1, 14,
  39, 14, 39, 76, 153
Erion, 2nd Lt. Don W.: 22
Ervin (B/39): 58
Evans, Pvt. Warren E.: 12
Farago, Ladislaqs (Am. writer): 153
Feil, Maj. Frederick C.: 42